How to Live
with the **Difficult**
Man You Love

How to Live with the **Difficult** *Man You Love*

You know you love him—now how do you live

with him?—as a husband, as a father,

as a friend

by Nancy Good

ST. MARTIN'S PRESS NEW YORK

Design by Judith A. Stagnitto

Library of Congress Cataloging-in-Publication Data

Good, Nancy.
    How to live with the difficult man you love / Nancy Good.
        p.   cm.
    ISBN 0-312-11421-4
    1. Men—Psychology. 2. Love. 3. Interpersonal relations.
    I. Title.
HQ801.G5915   1994   94-21199
158'.2—dc20   CIP

First Edition: October 1994

10 9 8 7 6 5 4 3 2 1

For Joanna

ACKNOWLEDGMENTS

Encouragement and support are always needed to bring a book from the idea stage to the finished manuscript. I have been fortunate to have several wonderful people who were generous and listened when I needed their support. Mildred Moskowitz, Lena Furgeri, Aimee Levy, and Debra Hertz were always there to say the right words at the right time.

I want to give hearty thanks to my editor at St. Martin's, Jennifer Weis, whose editorial comments, suggestions, and advice made this a far better book than it otherwise would have been. Thanks also to Todd Keithley for his help in the publication process.

My agent, Meredith Bernstein, and her associate, Elizabeth Cavanaugh, have helped to no end with their business acumen.

And as always, my love and thanks go to my own difficult man, my husband Wendell Craig. He readily provided his vital computer expertise whenever it was needed. Much more important, however, he is my partner in working toward an emotionally healthy and happy relationship, which is what this book is all about.

CONTENTS

How to Live
with the *Difficult*
Man You Love

Living with the Difficult Man You Love

*However, we must ask ourselves why there should
have to be any power struggle at all
between the sexes.*

—KAREN HORNEY, M.D.

ARE ALL MEN DIFFICULT?

Yes, all men are difficult. There, we've said it. No hemming and hawing, no beating around the bush. Any relationship that a woman is in, if it's not difficult today, will become difficult tomorrow. And of course there are degrees of difficulty. Some men are mildly difficult, some impossibly so. Perhaps your man is a great lover or a good cook; he may be sweet to your mother or he's wonderful with the kids, perhaps he's even a big money-maker. But you and I know that he's difficult, too. There's a large emotional payment that he extracts from you for the good that he gives you in your relationship.

Let's look at the following men to understand this phenomenon better:

Dennis is an intelligent and interesting man, but he works long hours and when home puts up a cold, distant wall. If his fiancée tries to talk about their problems, he gives her the silent treatment which can last for days. He says he's too busy to keep the house clean or to cook, and she realizes that their problems will only get worse if they have children.

Greg can be romantic and a wonderful sexual partner, but he's explosive and verbally abusive. If his wife becomes angry, he yells louder so that her complaints get forgotten. He also hates taking vacations, so any vacation they do take becomes a misery for her.

Joseph is a great athlete and takes exciting trips to ski, snorkel, bike, and climb mountains with his girlfriend. But the tradeoff is that he expects her to go along with him to local bars and take the jokes and insults that he directs at her when he's drunk. He sees nothing wrong in flirting with other women.

Jay is a talented musician, calm and quiet during crises, and terrific with the kids, but he's not interested in sex and has no career ambitions. When his wife talks to him about money, his colitis acts up so that he can't go to work at all.

Hank is fun to be with and sees his girlfriend every weekend, but he says marriage or living together is not for him now because she's not the girl he dreamed of. He gets depressed when she tries to break up with him and calls her until she sees him again. He doesn't change his position on marriage, however.

Charles cooks, cleans the house, and is really very sweet, but he sees his parents three times a week and someone from his family seems to need a place to stay every weekend. His wife is ready to leave him to get some privacy. He thinks she's selfish.

Larry is talented, financially supports the family well, and at times is warmly nurturing. But his depressed moods bring everyone down on the weekends when they're together. Larry acts then as if his wife can't do anything right, and he takes their son's side against her when she tries to discipline him. Larry says he has no problems.

These men are just like the men you know. They are not unusually awful. They are not physical abusers, and except possibly for Hank, they are not addictive types. All have assets that would make a woman want to be with them. Each of them has made a commitment to a serious relationship—whether it is monogamous dating, living together, or marriage. But each is stuck in a destructive mode of behavior that is making his mate's life very difficult. In most of the situations, the problems these men now cause for their women only surfaced after they made a commitment.

If you evaluate your own situation or that of others that you know, you will start to see the tradeoffs that women have had to make. In order to be with your man, you have had to give up something that is important to you. Perhaps it is a need to be really understood and supported when you're upset—something he just can't seem to do. Or perhaps it is giving up the wish to be financially secure. Perhaps you've stopped hoping that you can be happy with him and have just settled for existing with your difficult man.

Men have not become difficult just recently. We know that from cavemen to the present, women have been dragged off as a prize of war, burned at the stake, or branded with scarlet letters by fearful men. But in the nineties the absence of any kind of severe abuse in your relationship is not enough. Women are now beyond being grateful if their man treats them nicely at times. They want more than monetary support, and possibly because financial independence is becoming a reality, they want more than just to have any man on their arm who will stick around.

You know how you ought to be treated emotionally. You do not want to pretend that his verbal rages or silence or criticisms are acceptable because, after all, he is otherwise all right. You want a man who is aware of his moods and takes responsibility for what he feels. He should be able to hear your anger or anxiety or fears. You want a man with whom you can actively build a life that is rich and fulfilling for both of you.

Despite what we are saying about all men being difficult, you can create this kind of life with your man even though he seems to be a very difficult type. It is possible to get what you need from him. In this book, as in my first book, *How to Love a Difficult Man,* you will find advice on how to do this without sacrificing your pride, your dignity, or your identity. But we will go beyond discussing how to love him now. We will talk about how to live with him and have children with him.

Women need to be aware that they share a common problem: Their men act in more hurtful or destructive ways, are more difficult, with them than with anyone else. It is not your imagination, it is not your fault (although you may unknowingly be making the situation worse for yourself). When it comes to maintaining an intimate, constant relationship with you, the woman with whom they live or to whom they have made some sort of emotional commitment, men have problems.

Many factors predispose a man to making his woman's life difficult once the relationship is romantic. Much of this book will be devoted to looking at these factors. But cultural mores and society's daily demands and expectations on us all set up the situation in advance to be difficult. For example, if in a relationship women are supposed to be the emotional and nurturing ones while men act tough and cover up their real feelings, how are you ever going to be nurtured in return? Or if we consider the rigid roles imposed on women to be the homemakers and primary childcare providers while men stay out of the kitchen and the nursery, how can women achieve equality in the home or outside of it?

Then there is society's favorite myth that says men must be the head of the family and know all. In fact, men are often so angry about their responsibilities and feel so inadequate that they are precisely the wrong ones to head the family unless they become aware of these deeper feelings. In the chapters on fathering, we will look at how men act out their desperation in any number of destructive ways. Add to this the potentially strong negative influence of your man's family history on his psychological state; you can see that your problems with your difficult man were, like an accident, just waiting to happen.

We are trapped, it seems, by predetermined circumstances to have problems with men once we love them. Some women do unconsciously look for more troublesome men than others, just as some men do cause more trouble than others. And circumstances are better for women than they were, say, one hundred years ago. We are not put into asylums for trumped-up reasons by jealous mates or locked up in curtained houses waiting for the man of the world to return. But still in the 1990s no one, not even Cinderella, gets away easy.

My three-year-old daughter doesn't know this, however. She loves the Cinderella, Snow White, Little Mermaid, and Aladdin genre of stories. The important point for her is that the girl must get the boy. Then the story is a hit. Whether or not the girl goes on to be a success in her own right, to be financially independent, doesn't matter. Getting her man is everything to my daughter. It is certainly the subject of another book to determine why this is so. Little girls seem to need the myth that a girl only has to get a boy and she will live happily ever after.

But big girls suffer if they continue as adults to believe in fairly tales. When a woman can acknowledge that "happily ever after" will not happen like that for her outside of the storybooks, she is many steps ahead. To find happiness with a man and to be true to yourself always takes a lot of hard work. As the blissful beginning of any relationship ends, reality takes over.

Your fantasy may have collapsed, but it is not your fault. You still want everything to be wonderful. You want to be married and have children and that isn't happening. Or you already are married with a child, but this family life is not what you thought it would be. Your man has turned out to be not a prince at all, but a difficult man.

AM I DOOMED TO BE UNHAPPY WITH A MAN?

You may understandably be asking yourself, If all men are difficult, am I doomed to be unhappy? Does it mean that I have to choose between swallowing my anger about issues that have always bothered me, or nagging him for the rest of our life together? Or should I just stay away from men entirely? Fortunately, there is a better answer than getting rid of him or being dissatisfied and unhappy with him.

Change can happen. *Difficult men can get better.* However, the only way that change will ever happen is if you take the first steps. *How to Love a Difficult Man* was based on that premise, and this book is as well. But here we will explore in much greater depth your fears, his ability to provoke you to be angry, and his emotional issues that get worse when you live with him and when he becomes the father of your child. You will continue to find here massive amounts of support and ammunition to fight for what you want and believe because your confidence will be the answer to getting what you want from him.

You will be the vital key for change since women more naturally expect to work on themselves in emotional ways than men do. Women hope that change will occur in themselves and in the man for the good of the relationship, whereas men claim to want the status quo. Thus women not only have to work on themselves but they must also be the agents for any change that will happen in their mates. This is a hard job, perhaps the hardest of all. Harder than being a corporate vice-president or writing a novel, even harder than mothering. You feel as if you are in control at least most of the time doing any of those jobs. But your difficult man leaves you feeling out of control and unable to get what you know would be good for you and for him. You need help with him and with the relationship.

Let's look at Janice's situation.

Janice used to have fun with Tony, but not any longer. She and Tony have lived together for five years with no plans to marry. Janice would like to have children, but Tony won't even talk about it. In the meantime, Tony has been advancing steadily in his career as a chef, a career that Janice encouraged. She even helped him to find his present job at an up-and-coming restaurant. Perhaps because she helped him so much to begin, he is leaning on her more and more heavily. Every evening, closer to midnight really, he arrives home filled with anxiety about the day, his relationship with the owner, the constant pressures he is under. He threatens to quit regularly. Janice and Tony make about the same amount of money and need both incomes to live well, which makes Janice anxious, too, when he complains.

She feels exhausted from her own day but has to give him support and encouragement, and figure out how to deal with the owner. She loses sleep every night because of this. She has tried to get him to a therapy group she heard of that deals with work-related issues, but he refuses. Meanwhile, her issues about marriage and children are pushed aside. Her life with Tony is no longer happy. Janice has the man that she thought she wanted but not in the way that she dreamed.

Janice has built a life with Tony that seems to be filling all of his needs, but not any of hers. She feels like she is carrying the concrete foundation blocks of their relationship on her shoulders. Tony has special difficulties in the area of success, but he is easy in many other ways. Janice "pays" to have this relationship, just as all women "pay" in some way.

Janice can change this relationship. First, however, she needs help to understand why Tony has problems with work and marriage and to see that these are not because of her. She must decide that she deserves a reciprocal relationship. She will be his confidante but she wants to have fun as well. Tony must stop burdening her with his emotional issues and get some outside help. Janice also wants to be married. She needs support to be firm with Tony about discussing marriage, letting him know that she is not happy and needs more from their relationship.

Janice can learn techniques to help her disengage from his problems. A support group or other therapy will help her realize that it is highly unlikely that Tony will leave her if she changes the rules and asks for a reciprocal relationship. If he will not give her what she wants, perhaps he is not the man for her.

In a fair world, building a life together would mean that you both grow and change when it's time, reminding each other to do this while keeping your individual and collective emotional lines open to new communication, new understandings of what it means to be you and to be a couple. Unfortunately, life as usual is not fair and your relationship will not change in that way.

As resentful as you may be about being the one who has to take the first steps to get him to change, there is no other answer. He will not change unless you initiate it. We now know that all men are difficult, each causing their mate problems in their own unique way. Your man will find your Achilles heel—not consciously or on purpose—but it will happen. Why did you get involved with someone who has this particular set of problems that touch your especially raw nerve?

WHY AM I INVOLVED WITH THIS MAN?

It is self-destructive if you think to yourself that there is something wrong with you when you are having problems with your man. But there is a point to asking yourself, why am I involved with this particular difficult man who causes me heartache? When you ask yourself this question, you are ready to look at how issues from your past are coming up now with him and need to be understood by you. You can explore how he emotionally duplicates your family experience, what you are struggling with in yourself by trying to change him, who he represents to you.

Knowing the "psychological score" is the way I referred to this in *How to Love a Difficult Man.* You need to understand his psychological background as well as your own. By asking yourself questions such as, Is my mate like my father? Is that why I feel scared?, you can become an expert in knowing the psychological score. You need this psychological tool to avoid getting stuck in a relationship that never improves in part because you do not know about your own emotional history. You will find sample questions like this one in chapter four.

Sheila didn't know the psychological score. Zachary was sweet when he and Sheila dated the first year. But when they got married, everything changed. He said he loved her, but now he spent one night a week with the guys and always came home drunk. If she complained, he'd yell and tell her how controlling she was. He made fun of her anxiety about her job and was sarcastic when she talked about quitting and getting a better position. Yet he constantly told her she wasn't making enough money. Sheila had never felt especially confident about her work and now felt paralyzed to make a change. She couldn't understand what had happened to Zachary or how she ended up with someone like him until one day she talked to her mother about how he treated her. Her mother said that Zachary was always nice to her and suggested that perhaps Sheila was the problem. Maybe Sheila should treat him better.

Suddenly Sheila understood that Zachary was a lot like her mother: Neither of them took responsibility for their own problems and both found a way to blame everything on Sheila. The mystery of her dilemma became clearer. Slowly she began to stop blaming herself. She began to work instead on getting Zachary to treat her better and to understand the impact of his own family history.

Consciously or unconsciously, we all want to "fix" our parents so that the family story comes out the way we wanted it. But parents are usually not fixable. Then, we unconsciously find a man who treats us in the manner that our parents (or other family) treated us as children. We participate in recreating with him the family systems from both households with all their joy, pain, and upset. So you end up feeling as bad or good as you did at home. Perhaps you try to correct the wrongs from the past that are the same as what's wrong with him. But your habits and your negative self-image from the past hold you back unless you understand the situation psychologically.

The similarities your man shares with your family can be positive or negative or both. He may like to play tennis, just as your family did, or cook gourmet meals and invite friends over, something that happened often when you were growing up. But he also may tell you that you are irresponsible about money, which your parents said as well. Or that you are "not smart enough," which you also may have heard before. Or during arguments that he provokes, he tells you what a nasty, cold person you are, and this is what your mother used to say. Or he acts out by never being home or breaking dates, and your father either left the family when you were young or wasn't home much, either. Or he drinks too much—and your parents did, too. Whatever the particular criticism or issues, you've experienced this before.

This sounds and feels like a living nightmare to you, as patients of mine have told me when they wake up to the fact that this emotional mistreatment has been going on their whole lives. Yet now that you are psychologically awake, you have an important opportunity. Since you are still with him and feel "stuck" to him, you will, if you allow it, be able to overcome your deepest feelings and fears about yourself.

Mary came to therapy quite depressed because Alex didn't want to have sex and blamed her for their arguments. He would become cold and dictatorial. Her father, an army colonel, had also been like that. And her mother still blamed the children for her own chronic unhappiness. When Alex acted as he did, he touched what was already a raw nerve for Mary. She held inside her the negative impressions of herself she got as a child, at least her unconscious mind did. This was one of the reasons why she was with Alex and one of the reasons why she was still "taking" his criticisms.

With effort, any woman can understand that her man's criticisms, and those of her parents or others, originate with *their* problems and feelings that have nothing to do with her. Once you understand this, the bad feelings you hold inside you will diminish.

A POWERFUL MOMENT IN YOUR LIFE

Now comes a truly powerful and pivotal moment in your life. As a result of believing that all is not your fault and that you are really terrific, change will occur. He will improve or you will seriously consider breaking up. Because *you* are different and you can't be controlled by negative treatment anymore. These are the dynamics that take place:

1. You deeply believe that you deserve a better relationship. You know that you are not damaged or inferior.
2. He realizes that you have changed.
3. He tries to continue the old patterns that have made you depressed or upset. This does not work.
4. Now he either becomes more self-aware, more considerate in his speech and actions, more motivated to change, or
5. He knows he will lose you.

This does not happen after one week and not necessarily even after one year. But with a strong support network for you, a determination to become aware of the psychological currents under the surface, and the use of the techniques and dialogues described here, you can get the life you want with your difficult man.

WHY ARE MEN SO DIFFICULT WITH THEIR WOMEN?

Let's look at Eileen and Tracy.

Eileen has a deadline at work and has to work at home on Saturday. Friday night she asks Andrew if he'll watch their son on Saturday so she can work. "Don't you think I'm busy, too? Or is nothing I do important around here?" he yells back. Eileen is furious at him but confused. His work always comes first. Where did he get the idea he wasn't important? She tries to make him feel better and is upset all day because this has happened before. She does get some time to work on Saturday, maybe half of what she needed, but she's upset and can't really concentrate anyway.

Tracy and Nat usually discuss their schedules before they leave for work in the morning. This morning, however, when Tracy asks Nat when he'll be home he says, "You're checking up on me again." When she asks him the next day about what plans they'll make for the weekend, he says, "Why bother to ask me? We always do what you say anyway." Tracy is hurt. She didn't want to tell him what to do. She wanted them to plan something together, but Nat never says what he wants. How is that her fault?

Are these women really so powerful and is what they said or did anything that should evoke such tremendously negative responses from their men? Obviously not. And these men are not unusual. So we have to ask, what is behind all this negativity? Why are men so difficult to live with and love?

What Eileen and Tracy and all women face in their love lives is what psychoanalysts call "transference distortion." He accuses you of being "preachy, nagging, a witch, a bitch, a castrating controlling female." Or he silently punishes you for days for a slight argument or imagined insult. Or after three months of enjoyable dating, you tell him how much you like him and then he turns cold toward you and ends it.

Your man "transfers" onto you the feelings and thoughts that he unconsciously harbors toward his mother (and others) from long ago. Dorothy Dinnerstein, a well-known analyst and author, clearly says, "The earliest roots of anatagonism to women lie in the period before the infant has any clear idea where the self ends and the outside world begins."

Ms. Dinnerstein is talking about the first months of life. Maybe you can't buy that your man is impossible with you because of what happened when he was six months old. Perhaps you can agree, however, that what happened between him and his mother when he was three or four or ten years old does influence how he is with you today.

Let's look at how Nancy Chodorow, a groundbreaking psychologist, explains the psychological roots of men's intimacy problems with women in their adult years:

> Maleness is more conflictual and more problematic . . . because of a primary oneness and identification with his mother, a primary femaleness, a boy's and man's core gender identity itself . . . is an issue. A boy must learn his gender identity as being not-female, or not-mother.

A man must prove he is "not-female," "not-mother." Suddenly you may recall the many times your man did the opposite of what you would have thought was normal behavior. Men who said they would call and didn't, who said they would be there on time and weren't, who said they loved you but treated you far worse than they did their best male friend. And now you can also understand why this has *never been your fault,* even though you may have at times gotten caught in saying just the wrong thing. That is not the reason for the extent of his negativity. Patricia needs to understand this.

Patricia has been seeing Graham every weekend for three months. They've been having a great time, are sleeping together, and generally enjoying each other's company. Suddenly he stops calling. When Patricia calls him, he's standoffish, saying he has to work on the weekend, entertain business people. He'll call her next week. Of course he doesn't and when they do speak he says he doesn't know what she's upset about: Sure they'll get together again. He'll call her. And of course that's the end of it. No explanations, no fighting, only Patricia berating herself for having said something wrong, though she doesn't know what it was. Or sometimes being furious at how stupid men are, how hopeless relationships are for her.

Patricia needs to know that one of the important ways that men define themselves as male is by proving that they are the opposite of female: They must do the opposite of whatever it is the woman wants of them. Power struggles with you are secretly pleasing to them because these struggles are a sign of maleness. Most men are not embarrassed because they are "difficult." They are secretly pleased at their maleness.

Because women are the primary caretakers of children—boys *and* girls—and because all infants begin lives with a personality fused with their caretakers before separating to build their own identities, boys end up defining themselves as the negative of their mother, and accordingly as the negative of the other women in their adult lives. A girl can remained merged with her mother on many levels without fear of loss of her identity. But a boy is sure that to incorporate any part of his mother is certain death to his identity—sexual and otherwise.

Now, however, imagine a world where fathers are the primary caretakers and allow the infant to fuse with *them* in the early years instead of with mom. Then girls would have to define themselves as the negative of men, saying and doing the opposite of what the man wanted. In this imaginary world, men would want intimacy and women would reject it, men would want to marry and women would say no, men would wait for women to make calls that never came.

Just as some men are more difficult than others, some mothers are also more difficult than others—more invasive and intrusive, more controlling, less willing to allow their young son or the adult son to separate and live his own life as he wishes. As a result, some men are far angrier at the important women in their lives today. Instead of being angry at the mother who caused these problems, they are caught constantly in power struggles making their own lives and the woman's life miserable. Yet even a man with a better mother, one who graciously enables and enjoys his separation from her and who encourages a relationship as between two adult beings, even this lucky man will have to construct unnecessary power struggles at times just to prove he is a man.

An old maxim told to men, "Look at her mother and you'll know what you're getting," should really be rewritten as a warning to women. "Look at his mother and you'll know what he will try to make you become (and then resent you for it)."

Who is at fault here? Is it women again, only mothers this time? If anyone is to blame, we must include fathers, too. Men are equal culprits here as parents. Fathers distance themselves from the emotional needs of their family, are rarely supportive of feelings that would seem less than macho, do not make themselves physically available enough for day-to-day childcare. They pass along to their sons the problems they themselves have with women.

Biology is at fault, too. Biology determines that it is women who will be pregnant and responsible for nursing, thus becoming the first object for the child to merge with. But it is the culture and the rigid roles we assign to men and women that determine that women alone will be the primary caretakers beyond pregnancy and nursing; thus the primary figure to be merged with; thus the person that a man has to define himself as being "not like."

The role of men as fathers has changed in the past fifty years but not nearly enough. A father who accepts his own nurturing side while still feeling masculine, a father who allows his son to embrace all emotional aspects of his personality, a father who is involved in the day-to-day caretaking, this father should produce a son who has less need to define himself as nonfemale and who will have fewer problems in his adult intimate relationships with women.

That is one of many reasons for the special section on having a child with a difficult man—to advise women on how to get a difficult man to be a good or even terrific father. So that the next generation of fathers will be different: emotionally and physically available. It also deals with how to get a man to agree to be a father in the first place (and how to make your own difficult decision about having a child).

Children of the following generations should not have to suffer the terribly painful repercussions of not having two real, emotionally healthy and involved parents. Equally important, however, if we right now involve men in a full way in child raising, today's young boys don't have to become the difficult men of tomorrow. And the question "Are all men difficult?" could then be answered, "No. Some men enjoy intimacy without feeling threatened and controlled. They are full partners without prior negative patterning toward women."

IS THERE EVER A TIME WHEN A WOMAN SHOULD LEAVE?

This is another often-asked question. Ultimately, each woman has to make her own decision. There are no right or wrong answers. However, leaving a relationship before you've even tried to work on the problems can lead to encountering similar issues with the next man. Then you may regret that you didn't at least try with the one you've got now. However, there are three specific situations that are too destructive to stay with.

THREE ESPECIALLY DESTRUCTIVE MEN

First, there are physically abusive men. Physical abuse should never be tolerated. The first incident has to be the last one. Counseling is mandatory; nothing will change without it. No amount of good intentions on his part (or yours) will change this pattern without therapeutic help. If he won't seek help, leave. Any woman who finds herself in this situation also must seek counseling. You sought him out for unconscious reasons originating somewhere in your past, and it is absolutely necessary that you understand your psychological history so that you do not continue to repeat the past in the present. Therapy or a supportive group is the key also to give you the self-confidence and understanding you need in order to break away from being dependent on an abusive person.

Then there are men who are active addicts—whether to drugs, alcohol, or gambling. They are "serious acter-outers" who can eventually endanger your emotional well-being and your physical health.

Often they are sensitive men who can be fun and charming at times, and this keeps you "hooked" on them. Making a commitment to a man who has an active addiction problem is emotionally suicidal. There will be no reason for him to kick his problem if he knows he can have you, too. If you do decide to continue to date a man with an addiction problem, make sure that you date others, too, in order to maintain a very important emotional independence. Keep a distance from him until he has sought professional help and clearly distanced himself from his addiction. You might look to Al-Anon to help you separate from his problem. Although I am not saying that you must leave a man with an addiction problem, don't make a commitment to this type. Instead, continue to look for other men while you keep him on hold. After all, he's keeping you on hold while he puts his addiction first.

Last is the man who doesn't want to marry but is maintaining a monogamous relationship with you. This is a terribly painful situation for a woman for whom marriage and family is a priority. Sometimes, as in the case of Susan, working on this issue can eventually pay off. In therapy herself to become more confident, Susan relentlessly pursued her goal of marriage to Warren, who steadfastly resisted the idea. When she became secure enough to hold true to her threat of breaking off the relationship, he changed his mind and they married.

But these types of stories do not always have a happy ending. Only you can decide how long to work on the subject of marriage with a man who says no. Obviously, you will feel better about yourself if you date others and look for a more likely mate at the same time. Or break it off entirely. You will certainly be able to meet another difficult man with his own set of problems—but one who is not afraid of marriage.

If your man falls into one of these three categories, it is especially necessary that you learn how to set and maintain strong boundaries. But setting boundaries is important in all romantic relationships. Setting boundaries and creating distance when you are not being treated well, yet opening your emotional doors when loving and caring moments occur, is a skill that every woman can and ought to practice in her relationship. We will discuss this concept in a later chapter.

CONFIDENT WOMEN KEEP THEIR MEN

After years of observing women in relationships, it is clear to me that confident women keep their men. Insecure women are in far greater danger of losing them. Of the hundreds of women I have worked with over the years, those who doubted themselves, felt the man was always right, did everything they could to become what they thought the man wanted them to become—they were the women who continually were mistreated by men and ended up being left far more often. But if you do not feel confident, don't despair. You can develop confidence with practice.

Sharon is an example of a woman who for years did not have the confidence to deal firmly with her difficult husband. Yet eventually she developed it.

Sharon was married to Alan for ten years. They had three children. Money was always a problem for them, even though Sharon worked as a substitute teacher as much as she could while having and raising the children. The problem was Alan. As a car salesman, he had never made very much money, despite the fact that others at work made much more than he did. And he was a terrific salesman when he wasn't arguing with his boss or getting himself fired. He was capable of making much more than he did, but he sabotaged himself somehow just when things looked good.

Although Sharon worried about money aloud to Alan constantly and juggled their finances, she never pointed out to him what she very well knew: He had inner emotional conflicts about being successful and needed therapy to deal with this. She had never even blamed him for their money problems. And certainly never threatened him. She had decided when she first met him that he would walk out on her in an instant if he felt pressured in any way, and she had always been terrified of being alone. Her friends, however, saw how much Alan needed her and the cheerful atmosphere she created at home. They urged her for years to push him to make more money, but she was too scared.

Being married did not give Sharon the confidence to take the necessary emotional risks with Alan. What finally helped her was becoming more independent from him emotionally and financially. Once she began working full-time, made more money than he did, and joined a counseling group for herself, she was able to confront him with the problems that he chose to ignore. Much to her surprise, he did not threaten to leave. He was angry at first but afterward seemed calmer than he had in years. He agreed to go to couples' therapy together, and his income has risen slightly. Just as important, he has not been arguing with everyone at work. Alan would not have run out the door if Sharon had taken this emotional risk five years earlier, but Sharon was not strong enough within herself.

Making caring confrontations and taking thoughtful emotional risks improves the quality of your emotional life and saves relationships far more than breaking them up.

TAKING EMOTIONAL RISKS

In *How to Love a Difficult Man,* we looked at the dictionary definition of "risk": "the possibility of meeting danger or suffering harm or loss." We found that women had to be willing to take emotional risks with their men in order to get what they wanted. This, of course, is still true. No matter what your situation is—living together, being married, having children, or just dating seriously—getting what you want requires a willingness to meet emotional danger and suffer emotional loss. The ability to readily take emotional risks is determined by many factors, courage and confidence being foremost. When you take a risk, you may not feel confident and courageous, but you are. Just as the lion in *The Wizard of Oz* developed courage without realizing it, so will you.

Here are the three primary emotional risks that women fear as they deal with their difficult mates:

1. The paramount emotional risk that you face and that everyone fears in confronting problems with their man is the threat of the end of the relationship.
2. But there is another risk that is also scary: His anger, either passively or overtly expressed, will seem so strong that you will feel as if you have lost his love. This can feel as threatening as losing the relationship.
3. The last risk is less obvious but on a deeper level just as powerful in stopping you from speaking up. You fear that you will act very angry (scream, hit him, say things you'll be sorry about later) and feel guilty or at fault afterward.

These are the three most common fears that inhibit you. If you can overcome them enough to take a risk with him, you will most likely get what you want or, at the least, feel better about yourself. Yet so many women still paralyze themselves in the face of conflict-laden situations. Because fear is so strong and controls so many women, the next chapter will deal exclusively with these fears and how to overcome them. Marriage, by the way, doesn't make women less afraid of taking risks. But financial independence does increase a woman's confidence.

STAYING WITH THE RELATIONSHIP: THE WRONG REASONS TO LEAVE

Creating a fulfilling life with a difficult man is like white-water rafting. You can stand on the shore and play it safe, but then you'll miss the ride. Yet once you've gone on the raft, you've got to hold on through heights and depths that can be stomach-wrenching. Your relationship is not always like this. There are serene periods, happy, secure, and enjoyable moments. But each time you take a risk and confront his problems, you have to be ready for a wild ride.

Any major change in your relationship can be naturally stormy. All changes bring with them a heightened sense of anxiety and tension; arguments are necessary. First dates, first sexual moments, making a commitment, moving in together, marrying, new jobs, children—each step causes tensions. Sometimes that step feels as if it will be the last one you take together. These are the moments when you need to hold on and not take any actions based on fear or anger. Karen stayed on through ups and downs for the whole ride.

James and Karen dated for a year before they took a new apartment together. James gave up his old place. Karen kept hers and found a tenant. After a peaceful month, they talked about marriage. Nothing went right after that. James was dogmatic about a prenuptial agreement; Karen was insulted. Karen wanted a large wedding, which James felt they couldn't afford. The arguments and fights were daily.

Karen thought each day she would leave, and once or twice she did. She was seeing selfish sides to James that she had never seen before. He feared she was spoiled and would always be overly demanding. Despite their constant doubts, they eventually got married because Karen realized that a commitment like marriage had to scare them both. She especially understood the origins of James's money fears because of his family, and she went with James for premarital counseling that helped to calm them both down.

Taking actions based on fear or anger during moments of crisis is never helpful. When the smoke has cleared, you can see what is left after the fire, what remains to build with, what should be thrown away. Building a life with a difficult man doesn't mean that either of you ducks out of the relationship for just any reason.

In this section we will look at often-heard explanations for leaving a relationship. But these are the wrong reasons to break up. After each reason that people give for breaking up, I have given my argument for why this is the wrong time or the wrong reason. Use these arguments on him if he's threatening to break up, or use them on yourself if you're on your way out the door before you've tried to work it out first.

THE WRONG REASONS TO LEAVE

Reason #1: I'm attracted to somebody else and have a possibility of a relationship there.

Rebuttal: People always look better before you're in a relationship with them. If you haven't worked on the problems in this relationship, they will recur in the next one.

Reason #2: I finally realize how boring, ugly, and mean he really is.

Rebuttal: He (or she) is not meaner or uglier than before. But now you're ready for something more, and you feel safer to experience your dissatisfaction. If you run from expressing your real feelings in this relationship, you will cover up what you really feel in the next relationship and one day wake up saying, "I never realized how. . . "

Reason #3: I'm scared that the rest of my life will be the way the last part of my life has been.

Rebuttal: That's good. You're not pretending anymore that everything's okay. But knowing that you want the rest of your life to be better doesn't mean you should leave right now. You have just reached the first big step toward change. Work on changing yourself and caringly confront your partner about changing.

Reason #4: We are too angry at each other. We're afraid of what we'll do to each other if we stay together.

Rebuttal: Hating someone is never a reason to leave. Everyone has loving and hateful feelings toward his or her mate. You both must learn not to be afraid of these feelings and to express them constructively.

Reason #5: I feel guilty around him (for whatever reason).

Rebuttal: Look into this massive guilt. Don't run from it. Punishing yourself is not helpful. This guilt has its origins in your childhood, which is why it seems so overwhelming now. Your partner is also helping you to feel guilty.

Reason #6: I said I was leaving, so now I have to.

Rebuttal: Don't let your pride control you. It goes before a fall. Just because you say something in anger doesn't mean you have to follow through on it. If you feel this upset, though, it's time to do some real work on this relationship.

Reason #7: I'm trying to prove a point by leaving. Secretly, I'm leaving with the full intention of returning because I think this way he'll change.

Rebuttal: Leaving with the intention of returning usually backfires. You're alone, you didn't mean to be. You didn't think this through past the angry momentum that carried you out the door. The mate who is left might just decide that he or she doesn't want to get back together.

However, the wish to leave for any of the above reasons *must* motivate him (and you) to take action within the relationship and within yourselves. The primary reason why 50 percent of all marriages end in divorce is because couples bury problems. Then the member of the couple who is fed up has one of the above-stated feelings and leaves rather than beginning the work of building a strong relationship.

If you are about to take any big life step together (from first date to first home to first baby, even to retirement), then expect a wild ride for a while. Loving and living with any man, while making sure the relationship is on a course that enables you to get what you want, is certainly one of life's greatest challenges. Don't let his difficulties and your fears destroy your hopes and plans for this relationship. In the next chapter we'll explore your fears and learn to fight them.

Two

Fear—Your Primary Obstacle

My father, I remembered, had no fears at all. In that he differed greatly from me. But he could not be called a courageous man because he had no fears to overcome.

—YAEL DAYAN, DAUGHTER OF MOSHE DAYAN

Women are filled with fears they have to overcome in order to get what they want. Men act as if they have never known fear. But as Yael Dayan says of her father, the Israeli general, courage develops only because a person experiences fear. So women develop courage, acquire it like a badge of honor, by living through their fears to get what they want from their men. Though you love him and have even been with him for a while, there are issues that you are scared to touch. (So is he, but he'll never admit it.) You need support to push past your fears, to build up courage to deal with your man, even on what you thought were simple issues and even though you've known him for years.

Here's an example of an issue that comes up at the beginning of all relationships these days. Women are scared to deal with it and need the courage we're talking about. Jane is in bed with Gary. She's known him for a few months, but they have just become lovers. Contraception is needed, and Gary suggested she use a diaphragm, which she has. Jane thinks to herself that she really wanted him to use a condom because she doesn't know who he has been with before, but she doesn't mention it until it is too late. Or she tells him but lets him talk her out of it. Or she forgets about it entirely until the next day, when she becomes frantic thinking about the chance she has just taken. Whatever her thought processes are, the result is the same. She has had unprotected sex. Why didn't she just tell him to use a condom?

Fear is the obvious answer. I decided to look more closely at fear as an obstacle for women after seeing the response to *How to Love a Difficult Man*. Women loved the book and often found the support they needed to begin to make changes in their relationships. But often, even if a woman agreed with the idea of taking emotional risks for change, she was still unable to move forward. Her fear was the reason. It was crippling her. In this chapter you will look at the sources of your fear and what you can do to eliminate its power over you.

Let's continue now by looking at women who have been living with a man for a while or are married but still have fears that control their responses to their men.

Julie dislikes staying at her in-laws' cramped apartment when she and her husband visit. Each year after the unpleasant visit, she resolves to tell her husband, John, that they must stay in a hotel the next time they visit his parents. This year, like every year, she "forgot" to bring up the hotel and instead was angry and miserable during the visit.

Tisha lives with Stan. When they're alone together they get along well. But often when they go out with friends, Stan will make disparaging remarks about Tisha, often in the guise of a joke about her cooking, her attachment to their dog, her housekeeping, or any subject that comes up. None of these areas is really a problem for either of them until Stan makes a joke or comment. Tisha either says nothing or makes a halfhearted joke in return, but inside she is depressed and embarrassed. Since she went to therapy, she has become aware that she is really angry at Stan but so far she has not told him how she really feels—that she's furious and even thinks of leaving him when he acts this way.

After ten years of marriage, Sonya knows her husband's moods as well as his schedule. So it is clear to her that something is going on in his life that he's not divulging. He was promoted at work recently and might really have to work longer hours than he used to, but he has also been distant, which is not like him. Sonya can think only one thought—that he's having an affair—but she's scared to say what she thinks. The problem, however, is not going away.

SOCIAL AND CULTURAL REASONS FOR YOUR FEAR

There are many good reasons why Tisha, Julie, and Sonya are afraid to speak up. We will look at all of them in this chapter. Since an entire book could be written on the subject, we will only briefly look at social and cultural pressures that for centuries have contributed to women's fears. Men have been, and still often are, considered superior to women intellectually, physically, emotionally. What that unconsciously means to you is that you are speaking up to your "boss" when you bring up issues with your man, instead of just talking to your mate as one equal to another. Speaking up to a boss generates fear, whereas speaking up to an equal does not. Anthropologist Mary Bateson in her book *Composing a Life* writes, "Although we are extraordinarily romantic about marriage, we are curiously blind to the joys and benefits of real partnership." Since so few relationships are in fact a real partnership, your fear is in part a product of this imbalance.

Physically larger, generally stronger, father is the head of many households. And if mom said that dad was smarter, better, and stronger than she was, you believed it, too. Once dad is revered in this way, considered to be the family's leader, all men are going to seem like leaders to you on some level and be feared. There are, of course, households in which mothers criticize fathers all the time, and you may have adopted this dynamic as your own. But when you criticize your man all the time, he becomes the center of attention anyway and it can mean that you're afraid of him, or of losing him. We'll look more closely in a later section at how your family relationships as a child have contributed to your present fears of men.

Also contributing to your fear is another historic factor—the economic dependence of women on men. Women still make less money than men do for the same work, and powerful jobs are still not open to them as they are to men. Studies show that as women make more money, they become more independent emotionally and expect more and ask for more from their men. As long as he controls the purse strings, you might be fearful about taking risks and speaking up.

Lastly, women have been told by society that they are not complete without a man and that they have not succeeded as a woman unless they marry and have a family. Men have never been given this message as strongly. The underlying message to you is that you are not as important or valuable to men as men are to you. This places you in a one-down position and of course results in fear when confronting this "valuable" male.

All of these social and cultural reasons and many more have helped to bring you to the spot you are now in. You want more from him and you want him to treat you better, yet fear stops you from getting what you want. You should not blame yourself for your fear, now that you realize the social and cultural forces that have contributed to placing you in a needy, childlike, and fearful position vis-à-vis your man. You do not have to stay in this position forever. You can learn to say what you think and need and feel *despite* your fears.

BUILDING GOOD EMOTIONAL HABITS

Fear inhibits you, paralyzing your usual outspoken self from saying and acting in your own best interest. Starting out in a relationship with good emotional habits is of course the ideal way to begin any relationship. Good emotional habits are like good dental hygiene. Just as you have to get into the habit of taking care of your teeth to keep them healthy, you have to get into the habit of verbalizing your feelings—negative and positive—and asking for what you need. Teeth don't stay healthy without care. Neither will your relationship. The hidden problems will start to cause you pain eventually.

Fear prevents many people from going to the dentist and having healthy teeth, just as it stops the three women whose stories you read in the previous section from facing their fears and conflicts. As a result, they are feeling emotionally unhealthy, and their relationships are getting worse. Julie dreads seeing her in-laws and has petty fights with her husband because she is scared to deal with the real issue of staying in a hotel; Tisha doesn't stop her husband from being critical, so she becomes more and more depressed and her fragile self-esteem fades; Sonya thinks she looks old and unattractive and may be in danger of losing her marriage unless she stops her husband, who is on his way to having an affair.

There is nothing wrong with you if you feel fear. You are not a "wimp" or a "wuss" or a "baby." You are not an inferior woman or human being because you are fearful. Fear is a normal response to danger in the animal kingdom, and because we have a more developed brain, humans develop fears for psychological as well as physical dangers. Fears can, however, handicap you or stop you completely from acting strong and confident with your man when you need to, when it is important to get him to make changes. You will probably never eliminate all your fears when it comes to men, but you can learn to control your fears instead of letting them control you. The true danger to you lies in ignoring your feelings, fear being one of them. Your first step, then, toward overcoming your fears is to acknowledge that you are afraid and to know what it is that you fear. You do not *have to* take any action until you feel ready.

WHAT DO WOMEN FEAR THE MOST?

When it comes to men, women fear above all being rejected, abandoned, and left alone. It is awful to be left after twenty years of marriage; it is awful to break up after one year. No one likes to be rejected, of course, or even to have a relationship break up mutually, or to be the one doing the breaking up. But each woman has her own reason for being so scared of this happening that she will let the fear of rejection or abandonment inhibit her when she is with her man. Some women fear being abandoned more than anything else because they are terrified to be alone. You may feel scared or anxious when you eat alone, sleep alone, or go out alone. In other words, live alone. Others are terrified of breaking up because they blame themselves for whatever has happened and find it even harder in the next relationship. Or they feel guilty about causing him pain. Fear of being rejected or abandoned can bring up many fears from your childhood which add to the terror. There are many underlying reasons why a woman can be so afraid of breaking up, but the result is the same. She controls her feelings, actions, responses, her real self, in order to keep the peace and make him happy.

It was unusual and frowned upon for women, especially young women, to live alone as recently as thirty years ago. Thus it is understandable because of cultural pressures that women would have difficulty adjusting to being alone. The message has been passed through generations that a woman is not complete without a man. As noted psychoanalyst Clara Thompson tells us, "The official attitude of the culture toward women has been and still is to the effect that woman is not the equal of man." How could you feel good and not fearful about being alone when you are told that men are superior to you and you need them to complete yourself?

Cultural pressures, of course, contribute greatly to your fears of being alone. However, the most powerful forces causing the fears you have of "losing him" are from childhood. Later in this chapter, we will look at how childhood experiences could produce these fears.

By the way, just because you are afraid of being abandoned does not mean it will ever happen. In this chapter we will face your fears head on in order to overcome them, but that does not mean that they will ever happen. You and all women have at some time been rejected or abandoned or disappointed by a man, but it was rarely because you caringly confronted him on the issues in the relationship. The women I have worked with have found that their relationships improve over the long run and become stronger, not weaker, as a result of discussing problems. The man has not left them because they have talked directly to him about the problems.

There are, of course, men who will use any excuse to flee from intimacy at any moment. And they will blame you because you have "complained," brought up issues, asked for better treatment. But these types of men will abandon you whether or not you bring up problems. Ultimately you might ask yourself, how serious are the problems he causes and how much pain do these problems cause me? Am I sacrificing all of myself in order to keep him?

You may also at this point be feeling that you are inferior to your man because you are acknowledging your fears and he doesn't sound as if he would be scared if the relationship ended. But if you look beneath the surface, men act scared. They remarry faster than women do and die sooner if they don't. After the death of her spouse, if a woman does not remarry, she usually lives a long and healthy life. Men, after any breakup, often become ill or accident-prone until they connect with another caring woman who oversees their well-being. He won't tell you that he is scared to be alone or feels anxious when he eats alone. He doesn't seek help for his fears when a breakup occurs, not to the extent that you do. Yet he becomes ill, withers and dies—much like a plant. Or he might start to drink too much or act destructively in other ways.

Women seek help after the breakup of a relationship because they admit that they are scared and unhappy, and by admitting this to themselves, they guarantee that they will survive and be well. Thus it's important not to make the very wrong assumption that you are inferior to him. On the contrary, in the process of admitting to yourself that you have these fears, you gain more control and become stronger—superior, in fact, to those who deny.

Let's return to what you fear the most. Some women fear being abandoned not because they are afraid to be alone but because they always blame themselves for the breakup, tormenting themselves because they decide it was *their* fault. Richard broke up with Glenda after six months, telling her he didn't want this kind of relationship. Glenda was abandoned and scared because she thought she had been wrong. "He left because I was bad. I said and did the wrong things. I should never have mentioned that I wanted to go with him on that trip to California." She says this and of course feels awful about herself. "No one will want to be with me because I'm too clingy. That's why Richard broke up with me. I was too demanding of his time." Glenda can find a new relationship, but she will act even more indirect about her needs, for fear that she will chase her new man away. Probably her new man will find some other reason to leave and Glenda will feel once again it is her fault. Glenda's pattern is to become involved with men who will break up with her and blame it on her. She will accept the blame each time and feel progressively increasing fear in the next relationship and the one after that. As a result, she will be completely unable to verbalize her dissatisfactions or even ask for what she wants. Men will sense this and make no effort to treat her well. But Glenda can change this cycle. She can understand why she blames herself, and she can face her fears of speaking up to men.

A THREE-STAGE STRATEGY FOR OVERCOMING YOUR FEAR

You can overcome your fears of being rejected or abandoned for whatever reason. You don't have to live silently with the issues that upset or anger you, or else choose to leave him. And he can change as a result because you have chosen to give yourself the courage to tackle the problems, using the three steps of this strategy to move past your fears:

1. Give yourself a pep talk.
2. List your fears.
3. Talk back to your fears. Be your own best friend.

Let's see how this approach works for the three women we encountered earlier.

Tisha's husband, Stan, made fun of her in front of others, yet she has never told him her feelings about it or even asked him to stop. Before she decides to face him about the problem, she needs to give herself a pep talk, much as a coach gives his team a talk before they go out on the field. This is the kind of pep talk Tisha should give herself:

Step 1: Tisha's Pep Talk

I have every right to want to be treated better, and I deserve to be treated better. Being criticized and mocked, especially in front of others (even as a joke), is destructive to our relationship. I don't feel as close to him as I used to. I'm not even sure how much I love him. He is not going to leave me. He needs me as much as I need him.

Step 2: Tisha Lists Her Specific Fears

If the worst happened and we broke up:
1. I'm afraid I'd never meet anyone else—and be alone forever.
2. I don't know what I'm scared of, I just feel panicky.
3. I'm scared of going places alone, especially parties and movies.

Step 3: Tisha Talks Back to Her Fears

First Fear: I know I'll meet someone else. I always have before. I really might like being alone for a while to get back to myself.
Second Fear: This sounds like a fear from my past. I can get help with this panic from a therapist. I don't have to let it control me.
Third Fear: I can always arrange to come and go with friends. I don't have to be alone unless I want to. There are so many single people out there. Lots of people do things alone at times. It's actually a good way to meet men.

Tisha will not stop being afraid of being abandoned for these reasons in one day or one week. But she can, if she seeks help from a self-help group or therapist, find out right away that she is not the only woman to have these feelings. Any fear that you have ever had has been felt by others as well. Fear of being abandoned or rejected is a primary human fear.

Tisha finally talks to her husband about the fact that he criticizes her in public and finds that her worst fears don't come true. He is angry and defensive and tells her she is imagining things and that she is overly sensitive. For a few days their relationship feels tense. Tisha wants to back down, smooth things over between them because she feels scared, but she doesn't. She notices, however, that when they go to a party the next weekend, her husband is careful not to criticize her. As a result, she feels especially close and warm toward him and they have a better time together than they've had in years. The problem occasionally resurfaces, but Tisha finds it easier each time to confront him.

Sonya's husband was staying at work later and later. She suspected that he might be having an affair, yet she rarely complained about his hours or mentioned her suspicions. She needs a pep talk. This is how it could go.

Step 1: Sonya's Pep Talk

I don't want to live like this anymore. His late hours are destroying our marriage, and I won't tolerate it if he's having an affair or even a flirtation. I'm strong enough to handle an argument with him, and I won't back down or let him make me feel that it's my fault. I'm sure he won't leave me. *He* ought to come to *me* to talk about the problems. He's lucky that I'm brave enough to confront him and don't just leave him.

Step 2: Sonya Lists Her Specific Fears

1. If we broke up, I'd hate sleeping alone. I'm scared and feel lonely without Jack there. It feels like I'll never be held again.
2. I'm afraid of growing old alone, with no one to help me.
3. I want to have children and if we break up I might not find someone else in time to have a family.

Step 3: Sonya Talks Back to Her Fears

First Fear: Being able to sleep alone without fear is a skill that I can develop. I know that there are other men out there for me.

Second Fear: I'm not going to grow old with no one around me. That's just a way of scaring myself. I'm not helpless. My life can be as full as I want it to be.

Third Fear: I'm a terrific woman and I know I can find someone else. Having a child now, with the way our relationship is, would be terrible for a child and for me.

Sonya's story had a stormy ending, but they did not break up. She finally spoke to Jack. Jack denied any affair or flirtation and stormed out of the house during the argument. He said she was a trouble-maker and insulting. He was sorry he had ever married her. Sonya became scared and was sorry she had brought it up. She called a friend who suggested they see a marital therapist. Jack came back later that night and had calmed down. They did not speak again about the problems until Sonya made the appointment for the couples' therapy. Jack said he wouldn't go and Sonya went alone instead. He is still refusing to go for therapy, but he comes home earlier. When he's at home there is often tension between them. Sonya is determined to get him to therapy with her because she sees that his anger and acting-out and denial are problems that he must work on and that she cannot solve for him. She has stopped blaming herself.

And one last example of how the three-step strategy works. Julie has been afraid for years to tell John that they have to stay in a hotel when they visit his parents. Here is the pep talk she should give herself:

Step 1: Julie's Pep Talk

Staying in a hotel makes the trip more like a vacation for us, and we deserve that. Even if his parents feel insulted at first, I know we'll all have a better time this way. They like their privacy and they won't have to fuss over us. And even if they don't like it, it's better for *our* relationship and that's what's important. John's parents have a problem with separateness, but it's their problem and we shouldn't make it ours. We're staying in a hotel when we visit my family next time.

Step 2: Julie Lists Her Specific Fears

1. He'll be furious and I'll feel as if I am asking for too much and that I've done the wrong thing.
2. It's unlikely, but if we broke up I'd hate being alone. I get so anxious when things are bad between us that I can't concentrate.
3. I won't have enough money to live on if we ever break up.

Step 3: Julie Talks Back to Her Fears

First Fear: I'm not asking for too much. This is not a big request. *He's* making it into a major issue because he's scared of his parent's anger.

Second Fear: I can always go for help with my anxiety. I know many women who have been able to be alone and stop being anxious about it. I know that I would not be alone for long anyway.

Third Fear: This is a good reason for me to take my career more seriously. I can make more money if I work at it. Having more money of my own would make me feel more secure.

When Julie did tell John what she wanted before their next visit to his parents, he was offended and said his parents would be hurt. Jane thought over her request, gave herself another pep talk, and stayed firm about what she wanted. Several unpleasant conversations were needed before he gave in. She agreed to make the hotel reservation but John had to talk to his parents. He kept putting it off and finally Julie spoke to his mother. She was not at all upset and sounded relieved about the plan. John was surprised but pleased, and their visit turned out to be a vacation after all. None of Julie's fears about breaking up or John's being furious were even remotely realized. He was terribly scared of his mother and he needed therapy—she could see that now—but he was not really an angry type. She decided that she needed to figure out for herself why her fears of him were so strong. They didn't seem to have much to do with the reality of her life with John.

You know the type of fears that have just been described. The thoughts that you have when you are alone, before or after a fight with him, force you to act weak when you really want to be strong, to take care of him and pay attention to his needs when you have needs that have been neglected for years. When you're away from him, talking with your friends, thinking the situation over to yourself, you feel your anger and you become angry with yourself for acting "weak" again. Fear is the cause of your contradictory behavior. Fear is the primary obstacle to speaking up and loving a difficult man in a confident, forthright manner that gets you what you want and leaves you feeling good about yourself.

Follow the three-step strategy. Give yourself a pep talk, list your worst fears, learn how to talk yourself out of your fears. And you will certainly feel stronger. The next step is to know how your family history affects you now, how it makes you scared at a deeper level.

You will develop a feeling of balance and self-understanding by understanding your childhood. If your fears of being rejected or abandoned refuse to go away and are paralyzing you, then you ought to seek help in the form of a support group or individual therapy.

In the following sections, we'll put your fears into the perspective of those early childhood years so that you realize you are not at fault to feel as you do. In another chapter we'll look at *his* family history.

YOUR PAST INTRUDES ON YOUR PRESENT

The philosopher Kierkegaard said, "Life can only be understood backwards; but it must be lived forwards." For you to go forward without fear, you need to look backwards at your childhood. The fears that you have of being alone, of being at fault, and of breaking up will suddenly not seem strange to you. The origins can be uncovered in your childhood and by looking at your family today. Your man is also contributing to your fears, but it is no good to say, "When he's not around I'm much stronger and more confident. He's the problem, not me." You have to overcome your own fears in order to get him to change. He will not help you unless you push him, and right now your fears are the first obstacle to cross.

There are general childhood developmental reasons why every woman, no matter what her background, may experience fear of separateness, being alone, of his anger, of breaking up, more than a man will experience or admit to these feelings. As infants we all, boys and girls, bond and merge with mother in the normal course of life. As we approach two and three years old, we begin to understand that we are a separate entity from mother. But boys and girls deal with this realization in different ways. Analyst Jessica Benjamin explains this:

> Boys escape the depressive mood of rapprochement and deny the feeling of helplessness that comes with the realization of

separateness. . . . The boy succeeds in this denial by virtue of his greater motor-mindedness, the buoyancy of his body ego feelings, his pleasure in active aggressive strivings. What [also] accounts for the difference . . . in rapprochement the father plays the liberating role for the boy more than for the girl.

The "depressive mood of rapprochement" means that coming to terms with separateness is saddening and scary for children, but that boys find approved ways in society to avoid these feelings: by being physically aggressive and by identifying and being with dad. They are encouraged to be defiant, to hold separateness as a mark of maleness, to feel good about themselves because they are "tough." Girls aren't encouraged to be as "motor-minded" as boys and are generally not as identified with the father. Thus by the age of three, the gender differences in dealing with feelings of fear about separateness and being alone have been determined. They can and are of course modified somewhat over the years, and a strong mother who enjoys separateness, a life of her own, as well as closeness will be a tremendous help to her daughter in avoiding fears of being alone, fears of men's anger, and so on. Any girl who has a father who allows her to identify with his career and aggressive strivings will also be more comfortable being separate and unattached.

So all women are starting out with equal handicaps on the issue of being strong, independent women who enjoy separateness. However, some families unconsciously go further and do serious damage to a daughter, while other families create stronger women. Let's look at Kathryn, who was unlucky in the family she had.

Kathryn grew up in a middle-class home in the Midwest, the oldest of six children. Her father owned a store, her mother was a librarian. Her father was angry and explosive or just morose throughout her childhood. She does not remember any kind word he ever had for her. He abusively criticized her mother all the time, which she generally ignored. Kathryn was also scapegoated from the beginning. Although a good student, her father would not give her the money to send her to college or for that matter to keep her well clothed. Her role in the family was to be brave and take risks to try to get more for herself or the other children from dad. And to be uncomplaining. Although she succeeded in minimal ways to get some material things from the parents, she was emotionally scarred for life from the battle.

Now we move to the present. Kathryn has been living with Jerry for four years. He makes considerably more money than she does, yet is always late in coming up with his share of the expenses. He criticizes her because she does not make more money and rarely has any words of praise for the way she looks or for the many things she does for him. She wants to have a child and he postpones all discussions about this. Kathryn feels upset about the child issue but weak. She lets him make her feel as if she is a spendthrift when she asks for his half of the living expenses. Kathryn buys second-hand clothes but helps Jerry to look his best for work. He argues with her but finally relents and wears what she suggests. Kathryn understands that she has very low self-esteem and that she does not stand up to Jerry the way she should. But she continues to be a giving woman to this man who is spoiled, nasty, and selfish.

How Families Hurt Self-Esteem and Cause Fear

Kathryn's past has directly intruded on her adult life and damaged her self-image. Because her parents deprived her and her father never said a kind word to her, she feels inferior to others and afraid that Jerry is the only man who would be with her. She acts with him as if she is undeserving and afraid. Kathryn did have cousins who were kind to her and became successful, and from them she got a vague sense that she ought to have better.

Here is a partial list of the common ways in which parents create in their daughters a psychological climate that gives rise to an overly strong fear of losing a man's love, even temporarily:

- Direct verbal abuse
- Direct physical abuse
- Neglect
- Abandonment (literally)
- Withdrawal of love
- Failure to protect from danger
- Teaching that without a man you should be afraid and you are a failure

As a result of any or all of these factors, you are prevented as a child from incorporating inside yourself a healthy, caring, loving parent who unconsciously coaches you through life's difficulties long after you have left your childhood home. The kind of coach who tells you it is all right to feel angry, it is your right to be treated well, and that even if a man is angry at you, you will still survive. All women need this. No one has perfect parents, and only a fortunate few have even "good enough" parents whom they can call on to coach them when things get rough.

Kathryn is having a tough time as an adult because of her father's personality disorder—he is explosive, abusive verbally and physically, with a tremendously poor self-image—and her mother's passive-dependent personality. Dumping his problems on her, venting his childhood frustrations on this little girl (and her siblings), he almost destroyed Kathryn's ability to have a decent, happy, and fulfilling life. Over and over she does one good deed after another for Jerry, who symbolizes her father to her now, hoping and hoping that one day he will become nice (as she wished her father would). The occasional trinkets he buys her (never what she needs or wants) or trips he pays for are enough to keep Kathryn working on his behalf. She wants so much to be loved, and so desperately needs to be needed, that she cannot tolerate the thought of being without him.

Kathryn does at last succeed with the help of a support group and much effort in shaking off this past, and very gradually, she gets Jerry to treat her better. They finally in fact do have a child. But the struggle to rid herself of the fear of rejection and the even stronger fear (created by her parents) of not being wanted or needed took years, wasting much of her youth and leaving her little energy to build up a career that could have flourished.

Let's look at another example of a childhood that created fear in a woman.

Theresa is the second oldest of a large family. She was her father's favorite and often went with him to the hospital, where he was chief surgeon. To the community, her family appeared ideal, but their real life at home was sporadically horrifying. Her mother was alternately depressed or so furious that once she actually broke the oldest son's arm, twisting it in anger at him. Father was also periodically angry or withdrawn. He would kick the children if they did not respond fast enough to his orders. None of the children was allowed to disagree with the parents in any form. Achieving in school was encouraged, and they put the children through college. Eventually Theresa also became a doctor.

As an adult, Theresa was confident enough in her medical career but dependent and submissive with men socially. This became a real problem for her when she found out about an affair her boyfriend, Morris, was having with another woman. Theresa decided perhaps she shouldn't be angry. Morris convinced her that he still loved her but needed to continue seeing the other woman as a friend. Theresa went along with this but began to have serious lower-back problems. She was out of work constantly for the next year, and her staff position at the hospital was put in jeopardy. She became depressed and tearful all the time, blaming herself for not being strong enough to snap out of this physical and emotional state.

At the age of twenty-nine, Theresa is feeling the full impact of her childhood on her adult life. Her now-chronic back problems are a direct result of suppressing her rage toward Morris and accommodating herself to an intolerable situation because she is so afraid of losing him. Her fears and inability to feel angry are problems created in her completely by her parents. Both parents mistreated the children physically. Theresa's mother withdrew her love, especially from the girls, and verbally criticized them, suppressing all of the children's real and honest emotions. Even as an adult,

Theresa thought she must have deserved being hit. She never felt angry or imagined that hitting and kicking children was a form of child abuse. Theresa became a polite performer in the world, as her parents wanted, ready and waiting to be mistreated by men and lacking any skills to protect herself. She is terrified that love will be withdrawn or she will be hurt physically if she "misbehaves." Therefore she is fearful to speak up on her own behalf except in the one area in which she received encouragement from her father—the medical profession.

A fellow doctor finally talked firmly to Theresa and scared her into realizing that she needed help. Theresa went to a therapist for individual and group therapy, where she was immediately confronted by her complete lack of appropriate anger toward Morris. She admitted how totally afraid she was of losing him. With the group's support, she told Morris she would not tolerate his relationship with the other woman, no matter what he labeled it. She said she would not see him until he resolved the issue. This was a rough time for her, but her back problems improved with each passing week and she returned to work full-time. Morris eventually did break off with the other woman, and he and Theresa resumed their monogamous relationship. Morris coincidentally made his decision to be with Theresa after he realized that she was dating others and that he might lose her.

When you behave with a man as if you are afraid of losing him or as if you are afraid that he will be angry at you, you will usually be mistreated. Fear is the number one obstacle to getting what you want from your man, whether you have just met him or have known him for thirty years. We have seen that fear has many sources:

- Early separation issues with mother
- Social and cultural pressures
- Psychologically destructive parenting

Fears instilled in you from your childhood can be overcome, as in the cases of Theresa and Kathryn, who overcame extremely destructive parenting and became stronger women. Using a variety of methods—therapy, support groups, and the three-step strategy given earlier—you can overpower your past and take control of your fears. You don't have to let them control you when you are communicating with your man. You can learn to say what you really need and want without sacrificing yourself to his needs. When your fear builds up again attack your fears with the following:

Fear-Destroying Statements

1. I am not a child now, and I do not have to silently take being treated badly.
2. I have the same rights as anyone else to a life without emotional pain inflicted by others.
3. The man who seems to be so important to me right now is not my mother or father or sibling, but just a person with his own set of problems. He can easily be replaced, even though I could not change my family.

ONE FINAL (AND DIFFERENT) APPROACH TO YOUR FEAR

In a mystery story, the reader learns to be suspicious of what is obvious. All clues point to the butler as the obvious suspect, so the smart reader knows that the real murderer has to be someone else.

Finding the solution to your fear requires the same type of suspiciousness. You think you are afraid of your man's anger, afraid of losing his love, afraid that he will leave you. This is what you think; this is, as far as you know, what you feel. We could stick with this obvious conclusion: Your fear seems to be the obvious culprit. But if we become suspicious of your fear, we may find that it is hiding your deeper real feelings: In fact, *you* are furious at *him* and really want to leave him or have him disappear, as many of my patients have stated about their men.

Extreme, intensely felt fear usually masks just as intense rage and anger. Unlike the mystery stories, your feelings of anger and rage are not culprits or killers. Your wish that he would disappear is only that—a wish that is not the same as reality. But deep in your unconscious mind, you don't know that. You feel that there is something wrong with your feelings, something wrong and awful about you if you have such a thought as wishing he would disappear. That is why you are, without knowing it, hiding these feelings behind your fear.

Pat has been married to Walter for three years. When they argue, Pat often ends up crying, Walter walks out of the house. Although he always returns, Pat becomes very scared when he does this and backs down on whatever the issue was between them. Pat could live like this forever with Walter. Many women do. They cry at work when a boss gets angry or criticizes them, they cry at home when their man puts up a wall. But Pat's life and your life can change if you investigate your fear and your tears more deeply. At the end of the investigation you will get a reward—your angry feelings. Writer and anthropologist Mary Bateson tells us in *Composing a Life* that for her, after she was let go from her university job, "Anger was an achievement, a step away from the chasm of despair." Anger energizes you, enhances your self-image, makes you feel stronger. Fear of your man in your relationship will always weaken you.

The stronger your feelings of fear, the more convinced you should be that anger lies underneath. The more you fear that your man will leave you, the more convinced you should be that underneath this fear you wish that *you* would leave *him.* And here is another strange psychological truth: You do not have to express the anger you find in yourself, or actually leave your man in order to feel better and stronger. It will just happen.

Fear is the first obstacle to loving and living with a man. It is the primary obstacle. Once you control your fears and feel entitled to have a better relationship, change can begin to occur between you. In the next chapter we will see what you can do with this anger you uncover within yourself, and how you can use it to get what you want from him and to get what is healthiest for the relationship.

THREE

Anger and Rage in a Loving Relationship

A good indignation brings out all one's powers.

—RALPH WALDO EMERSON

says that getting in touch with your anger helps you reclaim your personality, your creativity, your energy, and the love in your relationships. The "trouble" that Vicky worried about was definitely there but in another form: her low self-esteem and anxious feelings which sapped her energy. Both these problems disappeared once she became aware of exactly how her boyfriend and her mother contributed to her bad feelings about herself.

Let's begin then by examining the specific ways that men provoke women, either on purpose or not, to be angry. That anger which you may then experience as some other feeling—anxiety or fear, for instance—is bad for you. You may recognize your man in the following descriptions and realize that you have the right to be angry when he provokes you in this way.

YOU ARE ANGRY BECAUSE . . .

Dr. Joyce Brothers once stated, "Anger repressed can poison a relationship as surely as the cruelest words." The anger simmers and burns and finally explodes in some form of acting-out, in the worst cases ending in violence. So if your anger is not going to be repressed and is going to come out in a healthy form, you need first to become aware of what it is that is making you angry. When Gilligan and Brown studied young girls through adolescence, they found that "girls . . . show signs of losing their ability to know what is relationally true or real." The purpose of this section is to help you find out what is relationally true—how he makes you angry.

The following is a list of the more common ways that men make women angry in relationships:

1. He misunderstands you.
2. He doesn't hear, doesn't respond to you.
3. He criticizes in a destructive manner.
4. He betrays you.
5. He mocks you, makes fun of you.

6. He tries to control you.
7. He ignores what needs to be done.
8. He exhibits explosive, possibly violent behavior.
9. He gives you the silent treatment.
10. He blames you when things go wrong.
11. He is nasty in general.
12. He messes up what you ask him to do.
13. He is chronically unenthusiastic.

Now we'll look in detail at each of these provocative situations that women experience every day from their men. You may not realize that some of these behaviors are a cause for anger. As long as you decide to remain in the dark about what he is doing that is harmful, you will be powerless to improve the relationship. Which situation triggers your anger depends on many factors. For instance, if you were misunderstood as a child, being misunderstood as an adult will feel more intolerable.

He misunderstands you. Women are always being misunderstood by their men. You try to be helpful and he's furious. When he misunderstands you, you're shocked and blame yourself. For example, the toilet isn't working and he's trying to fix it. You ask if you can help and he says, "You have no confidence in me." In another example, Rachel knows that Sam really wants to get a job in publishing. She has an old friend who works in that field. She asks him if he can help Sam get an interview at his company. When Sam finds out, he is furious at Rachel for being "pushy" and "controlling." And for having so little confidence in him. Rachel feels terribly misunderstood and devastated by this. She tries to explain herself to Sam but gets nowhere. She does not realize that she ought to feel angry at him for misunderstanding her reasons.

He doesn't hear, doesn't respond to you. You tell him what happened at work: someone else got credit for your idea and never mentioned your name; you say how upset and furious you are. Your man listens silently and then asks what's happening about dinner because he has work to do that night. You respond to his question and forget your own issue. You may notice that you feel even worse than you did before, but you don't connect it to the fact that he did not hear you, he ignored you, he did not respond to you. Perhaps you eventually catch onto this pattern and begin to feel angry at him, or maybe you never do. You ought to.

He criticizes in a destructive manner. No one likes to be criticized, but when it's done in a destructive manner, it's deadly. Destructive criticism should make you angry because it destroys your efforts, your work, your ingenuity. Here's an example. Susan has been working on a Christmas mural for their house as a surprise for their two children. Her husband comes home from work and says, "I don't want this hanging outside the house for the neighbors to see. It looks pathetic." In another situation, Jane is cooking dinner, something she rarely does because of her work schedule. Her boyfriend walks in and says, "I suppose I'll have to clean up this mess you make." The men in both these scenes have criticized in a form that is so destructive to the women that Susan might give up on her mural and Jane will not bother to cook a gourmet dinner for them again. Instead of attacking themselves, however, their anger should be strong, directed at the terribly destructive tone and intent of the men.

He betrays you. It would seem that you would allow yourself to be angry when you have been betrayed, but often women blame themselves for the betrayal. Don't do that to yourself. Let's say your man has been flirting with another woman or worse still, he has had an affair. You should feel furious and enraged by the betrayal of the commitment to monogamy. Your anger should also propel you to get help with him to find out why this happened and to make sure it doesn't happen again. You might choose to end the relationship, but we will discuss later on exactly what you can do with your anger that will help you, not hurt you.

There are other types of betrayals that are less obvious. Tammy tells her boyfriend, Martin, how angry she is at her friend Beth. The next time there is a get-together, Martin lets it slip to Beth that Tammy is upset. This is a betrayal of confidence. In another instance, Tammy's mother is arguing with her because she wants her to attend a distant cousin's wedding and Tammy is busy that day. Her mother tells her she is selfish. Martin jumps in and commiserates with the mother about how selfish Tammy is. This is again a betrayal: he takes someone else's side against you instead of supporting you or privately stating his views to you. Your anger is appropriate. Dealing with this anger is necessary if you are eventually going to create the kind of intimacy you want.

He mocks you, makes fun of you. Beauty may be in the eyes of the beholder, but humor is in the feelings of the target. If it doesn't feel funny to you, then it isn't and you have a right to be angry. He also owes you an apology. Often a man uses humor unconsciously as a way of expressing aggression toward his mate. At other times, of course, he knows exactly that you'd get upset and says it anyway. Mac says to Rowena, "Is that the biggest size of jeans they sell?" as she holds up her clothes while folding the wash. She feels hurt and makes a flip retort but later realizes she's furious. Mac never talks to her directly about the weight she hasn't lost after the birth of their child, but he even made a joke when they were with friends about how "she'll be taking up two seats in the movies soon." You are justified in feeling angry and can use this to work on achieving direct communication between the two of you. Whatever feelings Mac has should be expressed directly: "I'm upset because you are still heavy," for instance.

He tries to control you. He always has to drive the car, doesn't want you to make any decisions without his approval, doesn't want you to go out with your own friends, tells you that you should or shouldn't work, should or shouldn't go to school, and so on. Some women go along with this kind of "father knows best" relationship and their sense of self disappears . . . until their anger surfaces. Of course you should feel angry when he tries to make you into a child, dependent on him. But he can only succeed at this if you go along.

When you become aware of your anger, it will give you the strength you need to establish control of your own life.

He ignores what needs to be done. John sees the dishes pile up but never pitches in to wash them, sees that his clothes are lying around the house but doesn't pick them up, knows that the plumber needs to be called but won't call him, that bills need to be paid but forgets about them. Martha jumps right in and takes care of everything so that their home looks good and runs smoothly, only occasionally complaining that John does nothing around the house. She is much angrier about this than she lets show. This is a familiar story to many women. You need to know it is all right to feel as angry as you do. Then you can express that anger and work on a plan to get him to cooperate.

He exhibits explosive, possibly violent behavior. Violence can take many forms, only sometimes coming out as direct physical abuse. You will feel fear if you are with a man who is physically violent (this is defined here as being any physical contact as a way of expressing angry feelings), but you must feel angry and take immediate steps to protect yourself, including leaving the relationship if he won't seek help.

There are subtler forms of violent behavior that ought to make you equally mad. George, for example, can become explosively angry at the least provocation: one of their children drops and breaks a glass and he jumps up, screams till he's red in the face, eyes bulging. Then he walks around the house slamming doors and cursing loudly under his breath. At other times he throws whatever frustrates him—a pan, a hammer, a clock. Even though he has not physically hurt anyone, his anger is violent in its fury and feels threatening to everyone who's around. They fear what would happen if they got in his way during these episodes. Accordingly, his wife has decided to stay out of his way when he's like this. Any woman who lives with such a man will of course be angry—even hate him. This is understandable because the man is terrorizing the household with this kind of violent expression of rage. You need to seek marital or any other kind of therapy to get support for your feelings, and to get him to change his behavior.

He gives you the silent treatment. Can silence provoke anger? Of course. Judy is upset with Bruce because he came late to her parents' anniversary party and then forgot to bring the present she had left at home that he was supposed to pick up on his way. She told him after the party how angry she was. He made some nasty comments and then became silent, refusing to talk to Judy except for brief, business-type comments for the next three days. This silent treatment is a nonverbal method of expressing anger that ought to make you angry because it is extremely controlling and leaves you no way to resolve the conflict. Don't let his silence scare you or make you feel you said the wrong thing. He needs you just as much as you need him, even though that wall he puts up makes him seem invulnerable.

He blames you when anything goes wrong. Jessica made plans for herself and her boyfriend, Jack, to go to a housewares show at a convention center (they had just moved into their apartment) and then to meet friends for lunch. It was raining when they left their house, and she heard Jack muttering to himself that this wasn't going to work out. When they got to the convention center, there was a line to buy tickets and Jack said in an angry tone, "This was a terrible idea. Why do we have to do this anyway? I suppose you don't mind getting us both cold and wet." Jessica felt anxious, as if she had made a terrible mistake or done something wrong. She was about to say that they should leave when the line moved quickly and they were inside the show. The show was interesting and helpful and they both enjoyed it, but Jessica was in turmoil, alternating between fury and sadness, because Jack talked to her in a hateful way.

When events in life do not turn out exactly as he would like, he blames you, verbally attacking as Jack did. This can be an even bigger problem when you have children, and that will be discussed in a later chapter. But whenever it happens, you should feel angry and not join your man in blaming you. He needs to learn to express his frustrations without making you the target.

He is nasty in general. Any time there's a difference of opinion, or he's in a bad mood or has had a bad day, your man feels it's okay to be nasty to you, his emotional punching bag. Using four-letter words when he talks to you is insulting to you and using an angry tone is also provocative, even if his words aren't nasty. If this happens infrequently and he apologizes right away, you might not feel angry. But usually the apology doesn't happen or it's a long time in coming, and meanwhile you should be feeling furious and not trying to figure out what you've done wrong "again."

It's not all right for him to suddenly verbally attack you: "Why can't you ever do this right!" or, in a loud tone, "That looks like sh———" or "This f———ing knife doesn't work. Can't we get one that works!" In a moment he'll act as if everything's fine and you're tense as a board. Use your anger to let him know this is destructive to your relationship.

He messes up what you ask him to do. Larry agrees to do the dishes or call the electrician or arrange the vacation. Whatever task he agrees to do, Norma is beginning to realize, won't get done well or at all. When the task concerns his business, his own friends, or a project he wants to do alone, Larry can be a perfectionist and never forgets anything. Yet if the task concerns their life together, he's suddenly unable to think or act. You say to yourself, "Well, he tried, how can I be angry?" But of course you are and who wouldn't be? Unconsciously, he's angry also about being "controlled" by you and is showing you in what is called a "passive-aggressive" form.

He is chronically unenthusiastic. Jason is like Larry in that he is never enthusiastic about any activity or task that involves being with Maureen, his wife. He seems to save up his limited store of enthusiasm for activities like playing ball with the guys or visiting his parents. Even going to the movies or on vacation with Maureen appears to be a chore for him. Yet he always agrees to go. Maureen is frustrated and unhappy. She is starting to feel justifiably angry about being deprived of his enthusiasm and joy.

WHAT DOES *YOUR* MAN DO THAT MAKES YOU FURIOUS?

The more specific you can be about how he is destructive in your relationship, the clearer you will be at addressing the problem with him and the better the chance that eventually he will respond. For instance, "You're horrible to live with" globally assaults his entire personality and gives him nothing specific to change. But "You don't talk to me when I say that we have a problem. Your silence makes it worse. If you'd get angry and yell, then at least I'd know what you're thinking" is better. Or "I hate when you use four-letter words every time you get angry. Please try to control yourself around me and the children" gives him specific problems to work on and changes he can make. Yes, these are only a few of many changes that he needs to make, and as far as you're concerned, his entire personality needs to be overhauled. But it is a start, as opposed to standing still.

Use this area as a worksheet and list as specifically as you can what he does that makes you angry. I have given a few examples to give you the idea and get you started.

1. Leaves clothes and other possessions around the house. Acts put-upon or angry any time you ask him to do any housework.
2. You're supposed to go out. He's chronically unreliable about time: at the last minute he has to work late. He lets you know when it's too late to make other plans.
3. He's condescending when the two of you disagree. He talks to you as if you were a child or inferior being.
4. He talks your ear off about his day. You talk and he says nothing, changes the subject, or watches television.

5. He acts rudely to your friends or flirts with them.
6. He "forgets" all holidays.

Your List

1. _____
2. _____
3. _____
4. _____

Once you've written down your reasons for feeling angry, your feelings will be easier to control and use in an effective manner with him. If you feel yourself getting angrier and angrier as you write, you need to ventilate your feelings with a friend or a therapist before approaching him about the problem areas. I'll elaborate on this point in another section.

HARMFUL WAYS TO EXPRESS ANGER

There are constructive ways to express anger and there are destructive ways. You can express your anger so that you get all the pent-up feelings off your chest, but nothing else has been accomplished. You can say nothing and feel depressed and tired or just be silently angry. And then there are ways to tell him how angry you are while at the same time telling him how he can change and what you want.

You're not perfect, I'm not perfect, and neither is your man. You will surely see yourself in the following list of what not to say or do when you're angry, but do not blame yourself for this. You will see his destructive behavior in the following list as well. What you can do when you act in any of these ways is apologize, if appropriate, and from now on try to communicate more effectively using the suggestions in the next section. He should, of course, do the same. Relationships that last do not survive because there are never any fights, but because couples know how to fight, apologize if called for, make up, and feel loving again. They may do this over and over again in the course of the relationship.

Angry Behavior That Is Not Helpful

- You scream and yell and curse and use global attacking words like "jerk, creep, bastard, loser, user, horrible, awful."
- You throw things, you break things.
- You tell your friends how angry you are at him and why, but you don't tell him.
- You tell your children how angry you are at him but you don't tell him.
- You seek vengeance by having an affair, staying away overnight at a friend's, working constantly, spending a lot of money.
- You break up with him impulsively in the heat of an argument, then return a few days later.
- You analyze him and his family in a nasty tone because you're angry, not in order to be helpful.
- You bring in past history, everything he's done that makes you mistrust him or hate him.
- You give him the silent treatment for days.

Now that we've said that these behaviors are not helpful, I will contradict myself and say that there are times when letting your anger "hang out" does help. It clears the air so that afterward both of you can sit down without so much pent-up anger and really communicate with each other. It only works, however, if both of you get angry by "mouthing off." One of you yelling while the other receives this barrage silently will not work. Picture fighters in the ring. They want someone they can spar with, not an opponent who will fall down with the first punch and leave them feeling guilty that they hit too hard (metaphorically speaking). Even when you have a man who will verbally fight fairly with you, guilt can still be a barrier to your anger that needs to be overcome. We will look at guilt later in this chapter.

Passive behaviors are the equivalent of walking out on the argument. They are also not helpful as a way of resolving your anger. They are listed below.

Passive Behavior (the Other Extreme) That Is Not Helpful

- You act meek instead of angry.
- You explain yourself when attacked.
- You feel depressed, tired, or sick but not angry.
- You cry instead of getting angry; you cry when you're angry; you cry when he gets angry.
- You try harder to be understanding and nice.
- You ignore your real feelings.
- You feel hurt all the time.

Passive behavior is a way of attacking yourself. Maggie Scarf writes, "The fallout from this sort of self-directed attack is inevitably a drop in self-esteem. And this is . . . one of the primary symptoms—the hallmarks—of a depression." To avoid this drop in self-esteem and the resulting depression, keep alert for the telltale signs of passive, self-attacking behavior. When you feel hurt or are crying, you are in fact quite angry.

The last passive behavior, feeling hurt, is a feminine psychological tradition that has become a habit. Hurt is an acceptable womanly feeling; we picture the southern belle coyly glancing at her man batting her eyelashes, and murmuring, "I feel so hurt, sir." All of which should reduce him to forgiveness. But we no longer live on plantations, and men do not rescue women from their hurt feelings. Thus you are left with all your real feelings, anger being one of them. Hurt is the number one disguise, emotionally speaking, for anger. Although it is a feeling that does place some blame on him—you do feel hurt *by* him—it still is hurting you just as much as it's hurting him.

HELPFUL WAYS TO EXPRESS ANGER

Now let's see what you can do when you're angry that *is* helpful:

1. **Find a regular, objective source to talk to freely.** The key word here is "freely." You need to be able to say everything— "I hate him. I'd like to murder him. I can't see staying with him. He is so horrible"—without being judged, without being pressured to follow through on your words. You cannot do this with your best friend because eventually she will tell you to leave him or she will begin to hate him, too, or she will get tired of listening to you. In order to find an objective listener you must use either a therapist or an established self-help group like Al-Anon. A skilled, objective listener knows you need to ventilate with her so that the situation will improve at home. And she knows that you do not necessarily mean what you say. "Just talking" can have a powerfully positive effect.

2. **Tell him *specifically* what he does that makes you angry, furious, disgusted, frustrated, and so on. Use a recent example (like the ones used in the earlier part of this chapter). "I'm angry at you because. . . "** Julia tells Paul, "I'm furious at you because you talk to me as if I don't matter to you. Yesterday you did this in front of our friends. Your tone was biting when you disagreed with me. It sounded as if you hated me. Often you're sarcastic to me also. I think you need to get some help with your anger so it's not coming out so destructively at me. But whether you go for help or not, I want this to stop."

3. **Talk to him again about the problem when you are calm, but with the same intensity that you feel when you're angry.** Sheila and Lou argue frequently about Lou's long working hours. These fights usually take place after midnight. Sheila never brings up the problem at any other time. She forgets or decides that she doesn't want to disturb a peaceful moment. But during those peaceful moments you can communicate

much more constructively. Often you can negotiate compromise solutions: Sheila and Lou, when they did talk calmly one afternoon, agreed that he would be home by dinner time at least three nights a week. On other days they would meet for dinner near his job if he needed to return to work after dinner. Try having these calmer conversations in a restaurant or other setting away from your home.

4. **Tell him, *in the moment* (when you can), that you don't like what he's doing or saying. Try not to let these occurrences build up until you're ready to burst.** For example, if he is being nasty to you, tell him, "I don't want to be attacked. This has to stop." If he is being silent with you, tell him, "It gets me even angrier and makes this even worse when you refuse to talk. Nothing can improve this way. Say something that you're thinking or feeling as a start." You've told him what you feel and what you want him to do. If it's about housework, tell him right then: "Please vacuum, do the dishes, pick up your clothes. It gets me annoyed that I have to remind you."

5. **Strongly praise him when he is willing to talk and when he changes for the better.** If he seems cooperative or surprised but at least willing to hear what your anger is about, tell him: "I appreciate your openness and admire that you can hear me. I'm happy that you're willing to work on the problem." Tell him that you feel closer to him because things will get better and that you love him. You should reinforce this moment. So often we pay more attention to negative moments than we do to positive ones.

SPECIFIC RESPONSES TO USE WHEN HE IS RESISTANT

Unfortunately, he will probably be resistant. This means that he will deny there is a problem or say it is all your fault, using one of the following responses or his own variation. You may then feel defeated and become silent. Yet you must know what to say in order to keep the responsibility for change in his court. You want to keep him aware that you will not be talked out of your anger and that he must work on himself for the sake of a better relationship. When you use the responses I have suggested below (or your own that are similar), you are defining yourself as a separate individual; you have made clear that the problem is his, that you expect change, and that you are not going to blame yourself or forget about the problems.

He Puts the Blame on You

He says:
There you go starting trouble again.

You say:
The problem is not going to go away if we bury our heads in the sand. I don't want to live like this anymore.

He says:
Have you been talking to your friend_____?

You say:
That's not the point. You should talk to someone else to get a different opinion than your own.

He says:
Sure, it's always my fault. Did you ever think it might be you who's the real problem here?

You say:
I know there are things you don't like about me also. That's why we need to see a couples' counselor to air this out.

He says:
You're wrong. I never said that (or acted that way).

You say:
It's not a matter of whether I'm right or wrong. I'm telling you I'm unhappy with the way you're acting. You've got to do something or we're not going to last.

He Acts Defensive, Tries to Avoid the Issue

He says:

I don't want to talk about this now. I'm in the middle of . . .

I'm not going to take this anymore (and walks out of the room or the house).

Did I say that (do that)? I'm sorry. It will never happen again.

Let's just forget about this and go have a nice dinner— wherever you want.

He says nothing at all. He doesn't talk for a day.

You say:

There's never a good time to talk about problems because they're painful. Our relationship has to take priority or it won't last.

Leaving is not going to solve the problem. You walk out when things get upsetting. How long can you do that? (Then reassure yourself that you did the right thing.)

Being sorry is not the point. You're saying that to get me off your back. You've got to understand why you do this or it will keep happening.

I'll be glad to have dinner but that won't change how angry I am at you because . . . and I want you to . . .

What you're doing is destructive to our life together. We can't grow unless we talk. I think you're angry with me because . . . (You will need support from others to endure this kind of treatment without running after him.)

He Uses Sarcasm

He says:	*You say:*
And you're perfect, right?	You're being sarcastic and I don't like it. I'm trying to understand why I do what I do and to know what I feel. That's what I want you to do.
So what am I supposed to do about this now. Kill myself?	Don't threaten me. And don't change the subject. I want you to go with me for help. We're in a crisis.
I'm doing the best that I can. Sorry it's not enough for you.	The sarcasm isn't going to help. I'd rather you tell me how you feel—that you're angry. What you're doing is bad for us as a couple.

He Breaks Things or Gets Violent with You

Gets violent with you	Your response must be to get away from him immediately and out of the house if possible. You must take immediate action to protect yourself: call the police, join a self-help group or counseling, leave the relationship if you're ready.
Breaks things	Stay away from him until he has calmed down. Bring up problem in a public setting.

You're not going to be good at this right away, and he's not going to change right away. Changes that last can take years. My patients at the beginning report that they let him talk them out of how angry they are; they get confused; they end up taking care of him. Don't feel bad about this. Your man is probably the most important individual in your life right now, and it takes time to see clearly what exactly he does and to be able to respond in a strong manner. Ann's man was especially tricky.

Ann was dating a man who should be called Mr. Slippery. He always seemed to be apologetic and cooperative. He would actually cry and say how sorry he was at the drop of a hat. He cried when he told her he felt so bad because he hadn't told her the truth: he was looking for a job in another city and might be leaving. He cried when he said that he didn't think he really loved her enough to marry her. Ann would reassure him and try to make him feel better. Then she would realize how insulting he really was being to her, and how furious she was at him. The moral of this story is that a crying man is not necessarily a man who is sensitive and open to change; he is not being good to you or giving you what you want, and he may be trying unconsciously to get you to take care of him. Listen to what he is saying, not to the sound of his tears.

Fighting in Front of Children

Having children creates more responsibility for a couple, and not surprisingly, more stress in a relationship. The kind of stress that men particularly add to relationships when there are children will be discussed in detail later on in the book. For now, we can say that when you have children you can be sure that he will not stop making you furious. Yet you don't want to yell at each other routinely in front of the kids since children get especially anxious about problems their parents have with each other. Since children have not learned yet that their own anger is acceptable and not dangerous, they think their parents' rage toward each other is dangerous, too. However, if you never argue in front of the kids, you have an equation that doesn't add up: children plus marriage equals more arguments minus opportunities to air your differences. What is the solution?

Briefly, having children forces you to find alternative ways to express your anger. Fighting only when the kids are *not* around might be the answer that upsets the children the least, but it's not a practical idea, considering that you and your man have little enough time to spend alone together as it is. You don't want to spend all of your few moments together arguing.

Expressing your anger in a more civilized manner in front of the children is the best solution. Children need to learn that love and anger exist side by side in healthy relationships; that important conflicts are discussed and not hidden; and that differences are accepted, although perhaps not liked, by everyone. Saying "I don't like when you . . ." to your husband when your children are there, or "You are really annoying me with that . . ." or even "I am angry because . . ." provides them with an excellent role model for how to express their own feelings.

You will be the lone parent modeling how to express anger until your husband catches on. At the beginning you may look like the bad guy, bringing up your angry or annoyed feelings. Remind yourself that your child is learning for the future that a woman and a man can be angry with each other and love each other, too. After there has been anger or tension, it is vital that you then make up in front of your child or change the mood back to a friendly one.

Children force their parents to become better people. You and your man have the opportunity to become the kind of parents that you wish you had. And to create a family where all feelings are acceptable. But women unfortunately feel guilty about harsh words that they use in front of their children. You feel far guiltier than your man feels. As if being a good mother means creating a world without anger for your child. Creating that kind of world is not possible or realistic and not helpful to your child who has to learn to survive in the real world.

Guilt, however, is familiar territory for women. And nowhere do we encounter guilt more often than when we own and express our very real and sometimes very angry feelings.

ANGER WITHOUT SELF-DOUBT AND GUILT

To be angry without self-doubt and guilt is one of those impossible goals for women that is nonetheless still worth striving for. Of course you might ask, aren't there times when I ought to feel guilty because I've been angry? The answer is no. Punishing yourself with guilt because you've been angry is never helpful or appropriate. Feeling bad, however, because you have expressed your rage in a destructive manner, is understandable and is a helpful indicator for when you need to apologize or change your methods.

Women rarely experience anger without feeling self-doubt, which then turns into guilt. Guilt in turn robs you of your anger. Jane, for example, has just gotten to the point through therapy where she can tell her boyfriend that she feels annoyed at him when he pressures her to have sex when she doesn't feel like it. But she tortures herself with guilt and anxiety afterward. "I shouldn't have said that. I feel like I was wrong. The poor guy. He just loves me and wants to have sex. Maybe he'll leave me." These are the kinds of thoughts that fill Jane's guilt-ridden mind.

Why does Jane feel guilty and so unsure when she's been angry and asserted herself? Why do you also feel this way? Sometimes guilt has its origins in childhood, when you were given the message that you were bad for feeling angry. You were ungrateful, somehow traitorous and dirty—much the same message that is often given to children about their sexual feelings. Jane was told this and now she feels as guilty about her anger as if she had engaged in forbidden sex.

But women feel guilty about their anger even without such destructive childhood messages; we're not supposed to feel anger toward our men, bosses, children, mothers, or friends. We even feel guilty over perfectly justifiable expressions of anger, such as: "I'm angry because you're late. I'm angry because you're not dressed yet. I'm angry because you didn't do the dishes." These seem like reasonable reasons for a woman to feel annoyed or angry, yet we berate ourselves afterward—and apologize profusely. Imagine, then, the guilt that we as women feel about unconscious murderous fantasies we might have toward people who mistreat us. Or the guilt we have about our angry fantasies in which we imagine ourselves having sex with another man to get back at *him.* Or other angry fantasies in which we see ourselves leaving our man or seeking vengeance on him in other ways.

You might be surprised to learn that therapists consider angry fantasies to be an emotionally healthy mental exercise. If you feel guilty, you inhibit or destroy your fantasy life. This is destructive to you because fantasies are a wonderful way to safely let off steam, get back at him by acting out in your fantasies in ways that would be devastating in real life. When your guilt inhibits your angry fantasies, you also inhibit your ability to feel the anger you need to feel. All of these angry fantasies are normal, even good for you. All of your fantasies are desirable and do not indicate that you would in reality take action on them. Therapists find that the opposite is true: the more a person can fantasize destructive, angry actions, the less likely he or she is to engage in them. Your anger is not the problem: your self-doubt and guilt are.

Women are encouraged to feel guilty about their anger by society in general, which generally expresses a male viewpoint. It is commonly felt that if a woman has angry feelings she cannot also be nurturing, and society as a whole, and men especially, count on the nurturance of women. Dr. Karen Horney, a famous psychoanalyst, wrote in 1930:

> Males will always be in favor of motherliness, as experienced in certain spiritual qualities of women, i.e., the nurturing, selfless, self-sacrificing mother; for she is the ideal embodiment of the woman who could fulfill all his expectations and longings.

Thus a real woman should feel guilty about being angry because she has not lived up to the needs and expectations of her man for total nurturance. In the unconscious mind of men and children, there is fear if mommy is angry because it feels that this means a separation of some type is imminent. It may only be separation from the all-encompassing, all-accepting mother image—not a physical separation at all—but that alone is frightening and unacceptable. One can understand this fear in a child, but it is not acceptable in a grown man. When your man tries to make you feel guilty because you have been angry at him, he is playing out his childish fears and wishes. He wishes that you remain his self-sacrificing, selfless mother because he never outgrew his need for his mother and he still fears her. And he has now transferred those feelings to your relationship.

Once you understand that he tries to make you feel guilty about your anger and why he does this, you should be less likely to succumb to the guilt. The more you observe how the media and other aspects of society also value only a warm, nurturing woman and devalue an angry woman, the more you will understand why you blame yourself and feel guilty after you've been angry.

WHEN ALL ELSE FAILS: EIGHT WAYS TO THREATEN TO LEAVE WITHOUT ACTUALLY LEAVING

You have tried everything. You have been patient and asked caringly for what you need. You have explained what you think the problems are and told him how you feel over and over again. You have argued with him about why he needs to change. You have yelled, he has yelled. You have been silent for days or weeks waiting to see if he will try to help himself and the relationship without pressure from you. You have even gone for help to a therapist or self-help group. He still refuses to take his problems seriously. What else can you do except stay and suffer, or leave him and suffer also?

The bottom line for some men on certain issues is that they refuse to make any changes in their behavior unless they are threatened with the end of the relationship, with losing you. But you don't want to take such a final step, a gamble that you might lose because you'd be forced to leave the relationship once you say, "If you don't . . . then I'm leaving!" or be the woman who cried wolf. It seems like you are in another Catch-22 situation. But there is an alternative.

Here are eight suggested approaches to use which convey the message that you have reached your bottom line and that the relationship is seriously on the rocks without actually saying that it is over. Most men take these communications seriously and feel some anxiety as a result. You may have to "turn the heat up" in this fashion for quite some time before he decides he will make any changes—either to go for couples' therapy with you or to change on his own.

1. How long do you think we can last with you acting this way?
2. I don't want to live like this forever. You've got to . . . or we're not going to make it.
3. When you . . . it's intolerable for me. I feel so hurt and angry that I can't imagine staying with you and feeling this way all the time.
4. If this relationship fails it's because you refuse to make any changes or go for help.
5. (If he's been divorced or been through other breakups) Your other relationship(s) failed because you did the same thing as you're doing here (fill in what it is). You're pushing me away just the way you pushed her away. You're going to end up alone again.
6. I don't need this kind of relationship anymore. I've changed and want a happier life (more stable financially, more closeness—depending on what the problems are). Maybe you should find someone who wants to remain stagnant. If you won't make an effort to work on our relationship, then you're telling me to leave if I don't like it.
7. You're making a big mistake to give up on our relationship. You'll never find anyone else like me. I'm willing to work on

the problems and care enough about you to work on this and not just give up. Very few women are willing to put in this kind of effort.

8. We have a good relationship and care about each other a lot, but this one problem area is doing us in. It would be a waste to let this die instead of going on to have an exciting, wonderful life together.

He may respond to this approach with, "What does that mean? Are you breaking up with me?" or "So it's over and I'm supposed to move out" or "I'm not moving out—you move." He has misunderstood you because he is angry or scared, and he has decided that you have already broken up with him. Don't let this intimidate you and make you back down. Respond with: "That's not what I said. I don't want to break up, but it could happen if you refuse to go for help." Continue to use these low-key threats without breaking up or taking other action.

If I Hate Him, How Can I Love Him?

"I love him. I don't want to think that he's anything except perfect," said one patient. "Why?" I asked. "Can't he do the wrong thing and make mistakes?" "Because then I'll hate him. And if I hate him, how can I love him?" Tina was upset because in her mind hate and love could not exist together. In her mind a "Godfather" ruled. If she was really angry at a man, hated him in fact, then she never talked to him again. The only way to be in a relationship was to idealize the man and convince yourself that he was always right. That way Tina would never have to be angry with him and would never have to leave him.

As you have seen in this chapter, you certainly don't have to leave him because you're angry at him or even hate him. These are unpleasant but normal and unavoidable feelings to have at times toward your man. It is the price you pay for love and a relationship.

When the unpleasant, angry times outweigh the happier, enjoyable moments, there is work to be done and you need to use the more extreme techniques described in this chapter. But if you choose, as Tina did, to think he's perfect rather than feel anger toward him because he's not, you will subjugate a large part of your personality. You will not really be free to be who you are.

As with Tina, some women are so scared of their anger or anyone else's that they hide from it. You can always find the reason for this if you look back into a family history. In Tina's case, anger was expressed in explosions. When her mother got angry, someone would get beaten and Tina was terrified. You can see why she wanted to think that her boyfriends were "perfect"—so that no one would have any reason to be angry. Anger meant being out of control and she had to get away from that.

All of us have a little bit of Tina's feeling in us. We want everything to be perfect. We want our love to be unscarred by nastiness, by put-downs, by silences, by anger. It is hard to understand that a man who loves you can also be so "off the mark" when it comes to your feelings. But he most likely does love you. That does not excuse affairs, verbal attacks, never being home, or being angry and morose whenever he's with you. As long as you feel loved by him and love him in return, your love will withstand the anger that has to come with it when you decide that enough is enough. Deep love and caring really can weather tremendous storms and emerge to calmer, bluer, and clearer waters.

FOUR

His Family Connections

A child's independence is too big a risk for the shaky balance of some parents.

—HANNAH GREEN

All they wished for [him] was that [he] should turn [him]self into a little replica of them.

—MIDGE DECTER

The single most important cause for the problems you have with your man is found somewhere in his family.

Dr. Karen Horney wrote in 1967:

> The secret distrust between man and woman, which in one form or another we find so frequently, does not usually stem from bad experiences of our later years. Though we prefer to believe it derived from such happenings, this distrust originates in early childhood. Later experiences, as they occur during puberty and late adolescence, are generally conditioned by previously acquired attitudes, although we are not aware of these connections.

Like lemmings drawn to the sea, men are drawn to follow the conscious and unconscious messages given to them by their parents. Like lemmings, they blindly fall off cliffs due to their own self-destructive actions, never knowing that they have had no choice in the matter. There are differences, of course, between men and lemmings. Instinct pushes the lemmings; psychological messages from family push the man. And men are capable of changing their behavior if they become insightful: understanding the family messages and working to overcome their influence.

You, too, can be a lemming. You can be controlled just as unconsciously by your family. But I am assuming that you have taken the step to become aware of your family patterns and how they might affect you. If you're not aware of how your family controls your actions psychologically, becoming aware is a priority for you too as you help your man develop awareness. Most men are not aware of their family patterns—and don't want to be. As usual, you will have to start the ball rolling for his self-awareness and growth. This chapter will help you do that.

Here are two examples of women who tried to deal with their man's problems without understanding his family connections.

Georgia was worried and complained about her husband, Peter, who was ten years older than she was. He was moody recently, angry a lot, said he imagined running away from his job and responsibilities. He talked about taking early retirement when he knew the family could not afford that. Georgia thought that maybe a vacation alone would help him feel better. She mentioned his job pressures as a cause of his moods, or thought perhaps he was going through a mid-life crisis or male menopause. He needed to find himself, was her conclusion.

What Georgia did not look at was the real cause of her husband's crisis. Peter's father became chronically ill when he was only fifty-eight, ten years older than Peter was now. Peter was sure that meant that he had only ten years left himself. That was the main reason he wanted to retire so early. In addition, his father had never seemed very happy with his jobs or happy at home either. Peter imitated his father in that way also, never really being happy with his accomplishments even though he had a good job. Peter's mother had been the one he went to for attention and warmth. In order to get that though, he had to be "good" for her and make her happy. All the resentment he had toward his mother was coming out toward Georgia in the veiled hostility of his comments about retiring and abandoning his responsibilities.

Georgia wants to help Peter to feel happier with his life, but she is steering him in the wrong direction. Going on a vacation by himself or even retiring early will not help Peter's black moods. But an understanding of how he is unconsciously duplicating his father's personality will help. Peter needs to mobilize his anger about his father's depression and illness, as well as his anger about having to please his mother. He needs to become aware of these feelings and find a way to air them out so that he can live his life with a feeling of excitement and joy, no matter how his parents lived theirs. He will never do this unless Georgia guides him away from temporary Band-Aid solutions (vacations) and toward therapy or some other avenue of support to change his family patterns.

Here is another example. In this case, the woman laid blame on herself instead of understanding her man's family connection.

Susan was young when she married James. He adored her and was very possessive (which made her feel safe). He wrote her love sonnets and brought flowers. He couldn't wait to get married. Yet they were only in their "honeymoon" first year of marriage when he had an affair that lasted several months. Susan found out about the other woman, and he stopped the affair. Although they stayed married for several years after that, Susan never recovered from the blow. A beautiful woman, she worried about her looks from then on—and about her sexual performance. She never thought that there could be other reasons why James had had the affair.

Another important event also happened in that first year. James's father died suddenly, soon after their wedding. His mother, a difficult woman, was left as the responsibility of James and his brother. Susan never connected James's affair and the death of her father-in-law. It was many years later, after her marriage had ended and she had become more psychologically smart, that she realized one event had led to the other. Her looks and her sexual performance had never been the reason why James had the affair.

His family affects him, whether he is sixty or twenty, living near them or not. Weekly dinners with his folks (or yours for that matter) can provide an additional irritant, but parental influence is profound even if you only see them once a year or not at all. Tom and his father hadn't talked for ten years. Yet Sally, Tom's girlfriend, realized that Tom had learned from his father how to deal with conflict: he became completely silent. This pattern of silence that Tom had learned almost destroyed his relationship with Sally.

Families can be incredibly helpful or destructive. Parents also change with age and situation: As younger parents they may have been thoughtless and neglectful; as older parents they may become more considerate and helpful. Parents, like friends, may be supportive and giving in certain areas, such as money or dinners, but narrow in their perspective about jobs or relationships. Karen missed seeing that her in-laws were the real cause of her husband Carl's money problems, because they were so helpful to her. Her in-laws gave them money to help furnish their apartment and were very sweet to Karen. But Carl spent everything they had and they were always in debt.

The unconscious reason for this was that Carl was angry at his parents for being so controlling with him as he grew up, even over his choice of a profession. Spending money was his way of getting back at them. Karen needed to understand that Carl's parents, although helpful to her, were not helpful to Carl. With Karen's help and her suggestion of couples' therapy for them, Carl could begin to feel his anger toward his parents and not act on it by getting in debt. He would become separate from his parents. Let's look at what that means.

Separating from Family: You Mean We Should Never See Them Again?

When we talk about separating from family, this means an emotional separation, not a physical one. But what does your man have to do in order to separate emotionally? He does not have to *do* anything in order to emotionally become separate from his family. He only has to feel. As a result of feeling his true emotions toward his parents or other important family members, he will be able to set limits when necessary in his relationship with them. He will not be "fused or merged" with his family, to use two psychotherapy terms.

Being able to feel separate from one's family (remember, this doesn't mean that he stops seeing them; we're talking about an emotional distance here) depends on several factors. Here are the three most important criteria. If he fits into one of these categories, he might be able to begin the separation process:

1. He feels good about his achievements on some level.
2. He feels that people other than his original family (this means you, among others) care about him.
3. He has begun to feel the result of his own self-destructive way of living.

For many families, being emotionally separate, setting limits, feeling one's own feelings—these are considered acts of heresy. The 1930s movie *Now, Voyager,* starring Bette Davis, is a wonderfully vivid example of a mother who tries desperately to make her child live the same joyless, rigid, nonsexual life that she has lived. When her daughter separates from her emotionally (with the help of a therapist) and lives her own different and more exciting life, the mother almost disinherits her and acts as if she no longer loves her.

The threat of a parent's disapproval is so awful that most of us don't want to separate and understand what a parent did to us in the past and present that is causing problems now. But your man will not admit that. Instead, when you try to talk to him about separating even in a small way from his family, he will tell you that you are being pushy and destructive, talking psychobabble and being insulting to him and to his family. The smallest change can provoke this reaction. Nathan, for example, was angry when Ruth said that she thought it would be better if they did their own laundry instead of bringing it each week to his mother's house for her to do. They were, after all, living together and both responsible adults in their thirties. Ruth knew they would be closer as a couple if Nathan was more separate from his parents. Doing their own laundry was a sign to Nathan and to his mother that he and Ruth now had their own home. Although Nathan was angry and sullen for a while, he soon recovered and began to take more of an interest in their life together.

Your man may be unwilling or unable to set limits with his family, but he may feel relieved if you do it for him. Although this can be helpful occasionally, he will not grow as a result. You instead become his new mother, protecting him form the old one. Thus "taking on" his family for him is not a good idea, but he doesn't want to do this for himself. What is the answer? How are you supposed to encourage your man to acknowledge the reality of his family and become emotionally separate from them when he doesn't want to? We will look at answers in this chapter. Keep in mind that emotional separation is a long-term project, but one worth achieving.

GUIDELINES FOR UNDERSTANDING HIS FAMILY

Before *he* will understand his family background, *you* will have to; before he decides how to relate to them, you will have to come up with a strategy for dealing with them for yourself. Here are guidelines to use in analyzing his family in order to understand what happened in the past, and what they are still doing now, that makes him act the way he does. These guidelines are for your information only right now. Do not take the information you gain and give him a detailed report about how awful his family is. An important rule always to remember: don't belittle his family or analyze them as a way of getting back at him because you're angry, especially not in the middle of an argument.

Here are the most important questions that you can use to assess his family in order to understand where he comes from. These questions will seem overwhelming to you, so don't actually answer them. Just read through them a few times so that you begin to get an idea of how to view a family in order to understand the psychological heritage. Only one or two of the areas discussed will be especially important to any one person's background. After each group of questions is an example of a man who causes problems in a relationship because his family had issues in this area. You can use the questions to examine your own background as well.

1. What is his father like as an individual? Does he seem happy or unhappy, anxious or angry or relaxed, energetic or a sedate stay-at-home? What kind of work does he do? Is he successful or not? Does he seem happy with his work? Apply the same questions to his mother. Is either of his parents deceased? If so, how and when did this happen?

At the beginning of this chapter we looked at Peter and Georgia, who were having problems because Peter wanted to retire from his job and leave his responsibilities. He is an example of how a father's lifelong dissatisfaction with work and then his illness left his son an unconscious legacy of dissatisfaction.

2. How would you describe the relationship between his mother and his father? Is it loving and caring? Does one make fun of the other or is one nasty to the other? Is one parent passive and silent while the other seems to control the situation? Is one parent rarely home? Do they do activities outside of the home together? Do they have a social life? Do they celebrate holidays, exchange presents, and so on?

Sandra is angry at Bob all the time now because he is constantly trying to tell her how to run her life—what to do at work, what to wear, what accountant to use. More and more they see his friends and not hers because that's what he wants. He forgot to buy her a birthday present and bought her a small, thoughtless gift for Christmas. At first she thought this was because he didn't love her until his sister told her that this is exactly what their parents did at home. They didn't believe in giving presents. Sandra also sees that Bob's father tries to tell his mother what to do all the time, too, although she doesn't listen to him. Sandra is afraid that their relationship will end up unpleasant and without warmth. She's determined not to let this happen.

3. What kind of relationship does your man have with his parents? How do they relate to him? Is his father supportive and nurturing? Is his father competitive with him? Does his mother criticize him or tell him what to do? Does his father always have to be right? Does he have a silent relationship (nonverbal) with one parent but not the other? Is there a rift between him

and either of his parents? Does he relate to his parents around activities but not emotionally? Do they express feelings to each other? Are his parents physically affectionate or physically distant with him? Does your man idolize his father or his mother to the point where he does not see them realistically? Does his mother somehow get her son to take care of her but the reverse doesn't happen? Or is his mother smothering or controlling with him? Does your man support his parents financially? Apply all of these questions to both parents.

Tom is a sports nut. He watches baseball and football avidly. Barbara, whom he's been dating for two years, can't get him to go anywhere if there's a game and they've had many fights about this. And he meets his friends to play ball regularly on weekends, and Barbara has gotten tired of being the spectator there. But Tom is very smart, Barbara feels. And though he likes his job, he seems to have no motivation to move ahead. She can see that he's being just like his father with his sports obsession, and she ends up sounding like his mother, nagging him to go out. Tom's father is successful though, and at first Barbara wondered why Tom didn't take after him until she heard his father criticize Tom while his mother sat there and said nothing. No wonder Tom doesn't have the confidence to compete with his father in the success department.

4. Is anger ever expressed in the family? How is it expressed? Do they explode or give each other the silent treatment? Or are they nasty or mocking or critical? Is anyone physically abusive? Or do they actually tell each other that they're angry? Who expresses the anger? Who doesn't express anger? Does your man express anger the same way his mother or father does?

Greg makes fun of Sue's cooking, her flute playing, her friends. He thinks his jabs are funny; she doesn't. Sue thought that perhaps she didn't have a very good sense of humor until a friend said she felt angry at Greg because he ridicules her. When she visited Greg's family, Sue realized that all Greg's brothers and his father make fun of everyone. His father also gets very angry and yells every so often. Greg says that he'll never act that way. But Sue thinks that Greg's solution isn't very good. He walks away or clams up when he gets angry, which is exactly what his mother does. Sue wants him to be his own man, not a combination of his parents' bad parts.

5. Is someone in the family anxious a lot? Who gets anxious and why? Does your man express similar anxiety? How is the anxiety resolved?

John's parents are both anxious wrecks, as far as Joanna can tell. Yet John always appears so calm, which really surprised Joanna. Now that she's known him for a few months, she sees why. He only does what he's familiar with and doesn't take any chances. He can't even discuss the idea of ever moving out of his tiny apartment, doesn't want Joanna to touch anything there, and only wants to play chess and go to the movies. Joanna realizes he's carrying his family anxiety, but hiding it better. She plans to tell him what she thinks: that he's got to take more chances for their relationship to work. And that means he's going to have to deal with that anxiety he's hiding.

6. Is anyone in his family especially fearful? About what? Is your man fearful also?

Until they had a child, Harriet didn't know that Wade had any fears at all. But once their son Jason arrived, Wade tried to restrict his son's activity all the time because he was so afraid he'd hurt himself. Harriet wanted Jason to be active, to climb, to run, to be a little adventurous. Harriet and Wade argued often about how much freedom to allow Jason, and Wade criticized Harriet every time Wade took typical toddler spills. Harriet sees now that Wade is really a very fearful (and judgmental) man. She thinks his father was probably the same.

7. Does anyone in the family get sick a lot? Does it look as if illness might be used as a way of avoiding feelings? Is illness perhaps used as a way of getting attention and concern?

Jonas is healthy, but his brother Saul is always getting sick with a cold or flu, or spraining a wrist or ankle. When his mother isn't running in to take care of Saul, Jonas is supposed

to. Sonja, Jonas's girlfriend, is getting pretty tired of being a
nursemaid to Saul. In the six months she's dated Jonas, they've
spent a number of evenings with his brother, bringing him food
and so on. Sonja can see that in this family, you don't get
attention unless you're sick. She wonders if Jonas will start
getting sick to get attention from her someday.

8. Does the family eat to excess, drink alcohol, or abuse other
   substances, perhaps as a way of sedating feelings that are upsetting? Does your man do the same?

   Nora worried about the drinking issue with Rafael from the
   day she met his family. The family tradition was to have wine
   with every meal, and that's what they did every week when she
   and Rafael went there. But Rafael could hold his liquor: He
   never acted drunk, so Nora didn't realize how much he'd had
   to drink. After three years now of living together and with their
   wedding date set, she sees that the whole family really has an
   alcoholism problem. She sees that Rafael, like his family, uses
   alcohol to act as if everything is great all the time. They cover
   up all their real feelings.

9. What is the relationship between your man and his siblings?
   Are they older or younger? Was one sibling obviously the
   leader? Is anyone more successful than the others? Where does
   your man stand in this? Are they close or distant? Are they
   competitive but supportive of each other? Are they competitive
   and jealous of each other?

   Helen and George work for the same bank—that's how they
   met. And George is very competitive with Helen. She got a
   bigger raise than he did, and he sulked for a week. He said he
   was happy for her but his sulking took away from Helen's happiness. George sulks if he loses at any game he plays. He
   reminds Helen of a little kid because he doesn't share his
   things either—even down to the toothpaste that she needed
   when they went away for a weekend. He says his mother always
   forced him to share everything he had with his five sisters and
   brothers, and he still resents it. She was endlessly comparing
   how each of them did at school. Helen understands that George

treats her as if she is one of his sisters and as if he is still living at home. He is angry about sharing and wants to do better than Helen to get his parents' approval. George realized these family connections, too, as he was telling her. Things have been better since then.

"I don't want to become his therapist," one of my patients said to me. And she was right. Although women are the emotional caretakers of most relationships, the purpose of understanding how his family has impacted on him is not so that you become his therapist. Becoming his "in-house" therapist causes resentment on his side and on yours. Instead, the knowledge you gain about his family should:

- help you in dealing with him
- help you in guiding him to some self-awareness about why he acts the way he does (and perhaps into therapy)
- help you realize that it is not your fault that he acts the way he does: his family created him, not you.

"Too much knowledge is a dangerous thing," goes the ancient proverb, and you may agree at this moment. Now that you know where his problems originate, that they were created by such powerful people as his parents, you may feel that he will never change. Yet none of us, your man included, can move forward in a lasting way without looking backward. You will be stronger as a result of the knowledge you've gained, though perhaps not happier for right now.

Thus you have made a study of his family and figured out why he causes you headaches and heartache. You understand him, but he still doesn't understand himself. And worse, of course, is that he doesn't want to hear what you've learned. The emotional gap between where he is now and where you want him to be is just as great as it was before. And it appears to be impossible to cross from here to there, to where he will be aware of himself and his family dynamics. Like any monumental task, it may feel impossible. It isn't impossible, however, if you go slowly, deal with today's issue or problem only, and do not expect miraculous overnight changes.

A DELICATE BUSINESS: EASING HIM TOWARD REAL FAMILY AWARENESS

For the most skilled therapist, it's a difficult job to help patients become aware of the reality of their family and how that caused their problems today. And probably you are not a skilled therapist by profession. (Even if you are a therapist, it's not any easier for therapists to deal with their mates than for nonprofessionals). You will have many frustrating moments. It will make the path to self-awareness much smoother of course if your man is in therapy or comes to the decision at some time to do this. He will not have the same intense feelings, such as resentment, toward an objective outsider who tells him hard truths, as he does toward you; and so he will be able to hear more clearly.

Yet you are the person he cares about the most; you are the person he spends the most time with. Your effect can be enormous. One of the ways that you can help him increase his Real Family awareness (the objectively real family, as opposed to the myth that the family creates about themselves) is to be open with him about your *own* family.

If you think your family is perfect, he will not be willing to see his own as problematic. You can be a role model, showing him how to be open and flexible in your vision of yourself and your parents. Relate connections about your present-day issues to your past. For example, "I know that I'm scared of my boss because he reminds me of my father who was too strict with us. I feel like I'm a little girl again and powerless when I talk to him. I keep reminding myself that he's only my boss." These kinds of statements are ultimately educational, explaining a new way of thinking. The message is that it helps to be self-aware and is not threatening. We will see later in this chapter how a couple can create a support system in this way for each other.

Don't be open with your man about your Real Family awareness if he attacks you or your family with the information. For instance, if you said the above about your boss and your father and your man replied, "It's ridiculous to act like that" or "Why don't you grow up?" or "It's easy to blame somebody else" then this is a signal that he feels threatened by this kind of openness. Don't discuss your family anymore with him until he has increased his openness.

Another method for helping him to achieve greater Real Family awareness is to ask *gentle* questions or make "I think" statements. For example, "Do you think that our arguing about money has to do with the way your parents handled money at home?" Questions work best if he is somewhat interested in self-awareness. Otherwise he will respond negatively.

Making "I think" statements in a nonaccusatory manner is usually more effective. Here are some examples:

"I think the reason you're having trouble being successful is because your father doesn't really want you to be successful" and more strongly, "I think until you deal with your feelings about this nothing's going to change. The best way to do that is to go into therapy."

"I think you're confusing me with your mother when you accuse me of being controlling. You need to deal with your feelings toward her instead of taking them out on me."

"I think you learned from your family to give people the silent treatment instead of expressing your anger. I don't want us to live that way here. I'm not your mother and I want you to express all your feelings."

Even though you make these types of statements softly and gently, what you are saying is strong medicine and can produce a strong, angry reaction. That is why bringing in his family or using "I think" statements when *you're* angry will certainly not lead him to greater Real Family awareness. He will feel as if you are attacking him with his family's problems instead of helping him. Talk about these family connections when you are both calm. If he still reacts in an angry way, remember that this anger is only temporary. Although you feel as if you should never have brought up the topic, you will see results after awhile. Getting him to therapy (couples' therapy or on his own) is your goal so that you don't have to keep trying to explain these family connections.

Let's look at a woman who had a common but serious problem with her man—he refused to get married—and how she helped him to an awareness of the way his Real Family was interfering with their relationship.

Pauline knew Robert for ten years. They had been dating for the last four years. More than dating really. They had a monogamous relationship, staying in each other's apartments on weekends. Pauline was almost thirty-eight, and for the last two years she brought up the subject of marriage frequently. Robert would say maybe someday, or he couldn't make that commitment, or why did they have to get married? Pauline threatened to end the relationship many times but never really meant it. She knew deep down that he was scared to marry because he was scared of his mother, but she only threw that at him in anger during fights. Pauline had entered therapy herself a year before. With her therapist she had been looking at her own family and how they related to why she was still with Robert. Next she began to look at Robert and his family more closely, too. She found out that his parents had argued all the time, right up until his father died when Robert was eighteen. That was also the year he left for college. Because of his father's death, Robert returned home to be with his mother and went to a local school. It was only after his sister moved back home that he moved out. With this information, Pauline understood him better. During calmer moments she let him know what she knew about him.

"I think there's something strange going on here that we're like a married couple but we don't get married. I know it has to do with our families.

"I think you're afraid of marriage because you think we'll argue all the time like your parents did. But that was their life and we can be different. We can go for counseling if we have too many arguments.

"Maybe you're even afraid that you'll die from all the fighting. I think you think that marriage is death to a man. But you can tell me when you don't like something and if you feel I'm 'killing' you. I don't want anything to happen to you."

Pauline also was open with Robert about her own awareness of her family and how she had been ignored, hit, and deprived by her father. She told him that they had an alternative to living their parents' lives and that she was one of the few women who was ready to work with him on that. He became interested in what she said, although he was angry. At the same time, she worked on being able to leave him and told him that would happen if they didn't get married. The combination of working on his Real Family awareness and recognizing that he didn't want to lose Pauline made Robert decide to get married.

Even if you are not as successful as Pauline in getting him to act differently, knowing everything about your background and his will empower you.

SOME QUICK, PRACTICAL SUGGESTIONS

You want your man to control the situation with his family instead of letting them control him. But it seems like this won't happen for a long time. In the meantime, there are some concrete changes that you might be able to get him to make just by asking or stating firmly what you want without analyzing or interpreting.

Earlier in this chapter Ruth told Nathan that she wanted him to do their wash at their apartment and not to bring it to his mother's, where she did their laundry for them. Nathan had been bringing his laundry to his mother's for all the years he lived alone. Ruth knew this represented a tie to his mother that was not helpful to their new life together. She did not analyze the situation or explain it to him, but she did get him to stop the old pattern. And as a result, they did in fact feel closer.

Ann knew that Tony had taken vacations with his family for years. She also knew that this meant she and Tony would not have a romantic vacation. So she firmly suggested that they take a vacation without his family. She did, however, suggest occasional day trips with them. Although Tony seemed tense during their "private" vacation, they did have romantic moments. The family eventually got used to the idea.

Alice was furious that Sean told his mother in detail everything they did. She knew he was afraid of his controlling mother. Sean often took his anger toward his mother out on her. Alice decided to take a stand. She asked Sean to stop telling his mother about their arguments, her work problems, or intimate details of their relationship. Sean reacted with anger, but he thought twice the next time he spoke to his mother.

These are specific simple requests that carry a lot of weight in terms of unconscious communication to your man and to his family. You also get something in return immediately for the effort you put in. Although on the surface it appears that you are pushing him, the result is that he is more separate and thus more in charge of his own life.

WON'T I GET TOO INVOLVED IN HIS PROBLEMS USING THESE METHODS?

"I don't want to do all this work. These are his problems, not mine. I've got my own family issues to deal with." The woman who said this was angry because she felt burdened by my suggestions. This anger is understandable, especially if you "take on" his problems. But doing this Real Family work with him doesn't mean you do it for him. You're doing this for yourself so that he changes. Understanding his family origins should also help you to detach from his problems more.

Ideally, of course, you should not have to help him to be aware of his Real Family. Ideally, he would do that for himself because he wants to grow and change. But ideal men are rare, and if you don't show him the way to understand why he causes trouble, he'll never try to learn. He may, as many men do, continue to think that the only reason he has problems with your relationship is because you complain. But keep in mind what Dr. Horney stated at the beginning of this chapter: The distrust that he has of you stems primarily from early childhood experiences. Remember: How could you possibly be the reason that he acts so badly toward you—so angry, so depressed, so anxious, so obsessive, so stubborn, so insensitive—when he has known his parents much longer than he has you, when they are the ones who impacted on him from birth to the present. You are only entering the picture when he is an adult and already formed emotionally.

You should not help him with this task forever; you should not make him your life's work project. Eventually he will either have to carry the ball and continue the process of self-awareness on his own or you will have to stop working on him. In any case, Real Family awareness is only part of the answer to your problems with him. You will still need to set limits with him when necessary, detach emotionally and/or physically when he is behind an emotional wall, make your own emotional health your first priority, and always feel that you have the right to be treated well.

DIFFICULT FAMILIES CAN BRING YOU CLOSER

Jonathan and Debbie go for dinner at his mother's about once a month. Each time they visit, Jonathan's mother picks on Debbie every chance she can. She makes nasty comments about her short skirts, her "vegetarian diet," her frequent travel for her job, the way she tears lettuce for a salad. Debbie holds her tongue most of the time or defends herself. She fights with Jonathan afterward because he says nothing or tells her she just shouldn't pay any attention to his mother.

This time, however, Debbie tells Jonathan that if he doesn't stand up to his mother, she will leave. And this dinner will be the last. Jonathan hears Debbie and during this visit he stops his mother when she criticizes Debbie. But she then is nasty to both of them. Finally Jonathan threatens to leave and his mother controls herself.

Jonathan is able to acknowledge how bitter his mother is. Together, he and Debbie realize that his mother is jealous and lonely. They both feel angry and sad about her. But for the first time, Debbie feels protected. She also feels closer to Jonathan than ever before. And he feels grateful that he is with someone who is so different from his mother.

This story is a modern fairy tale with a happy ending. When Debbie and Jonathan finally get closer at the end, their closeness represents an advanced step in intimacy and emotional communication. But Debbie had to take a risk and slay some dragons before Jonathan reached that point. It may seem like you'll never get to that point with your man. But most men can eventually change if their woman insists on it, even in the touchy family area.

You and your man cannot change your families, but together you can develop a mutual system of support and comfort to help you both deal with the problems your families present to you. In order to do this, you both have to view your families without rose-colored glasses. We'll assume that *you've* already done this. We'll also assume that your man needs to be helped into this kind of awareness. We saw that Debbie pushed Jonathan with a direct threat. And it worked. She decided to use extreme measures with Jonathan because his mother was directly attacking her and nothing else had worked. Ideally your mate will begin to develop family awareness without being threatened. Once this occurs, the next step can be a greater intimacy than you've known before.

But that is not enough. You want your man to be supportive of you also when *you* are upset about *your* difficult family. That is the other half of this advanced stage of intimacy and communication, and it doesn't require that he be honest about his own family, just supportive of you about yours. When you are open about your family's problems, you want him to understand and be there for you as a good friend.

For example, Jan had not visited her parents in years because she felt intimidated by her father. When she moved in with Bart, he encouraged her to go visit her parents and went with her. Jan told him that she would visit them if he would be supportive of her feelings while she was there. And he was. He agreed that they were cold, upsetting people and he made Jan feel that she was not alone in her perception of them. He was especially nice to her during the visit, and they felt much closer.

Being close because you have difficult families also means "putting up with" each other's families to a certain extent. Your family may upset you in many ways, but they're still your family and the only ones you've got, so you still want to see them at times. Let's say, for example, that your man doesn't like spending time with your family at all and he'd just as soon not see them. But you want him to come with you to be supportive of you. So he spends a carefully decided upon amount of time with your family, which is a compromise for each of you. And you do the same for him—seeing his family even though you'd just as soon not. As a result, however, you feel closer and appreciate each other more.

Helping your man achieve Real Family awareness (the Real Family as opposed to the rosy-colored one) is one of the more difficult tasks you can take on, and one of the most charitable. Yes, you are certainly helping yourself if he changes in the way that he relates to you. And that is the reason why you undertake this task. But you help him immeasurably as well, and you should give yourself much credit.

Once he leaves behind the emotional family baggage, he will be free to build his own life and his own relationship with you unencumbered by the patterns that have bound him to the past. He can be successful even though his family was not, joyful though his family was not, healthy instead of sick, loving and close though his parents were not, able to make a commitment to you though his family secretly preferred that he didn't. You should give yourself credit for this when and if it happens, even though he may not really be able to acknowledge his debt to you because of his pride.

Your man needs to drive the long road to awareness of his Real Family by himself and take the turns of his own choosing. You can only try to get him to turn on the ignition key and point out the direction he can take. Once you've done this, you must let go.

FIVE

The Man Who Presents Obstacles to Having Children

*A son of my own! Oh, no, no, no! Let my flesh
perish with me, and let me not transmit to anyone
the boredom and the ignominiousness of life.*

—GUSTAVE FLAUBERT

Your man is in famous company if he has difficulty with the idea of having children. Flaubert thought life was too boring to be passed along. And George Bernard Shaw didn't like children. He said, "I must have been an insufferable child. All children are." These are not the kinds of statements women want to hear from their men if they are interested in having children with them.

Your man may make statements like these, or he may say yes but present other very real obstacles to having children. Because children represent a giant step toward togetherness, you may have to understand and overcome far more complicated problems than he's presented before in order to get what you want.

We will examine in this chapter how to bring a man's objections and issues with children out into the open. There is no better way to overcome these issues than to air them. Ignoring a man's protests against children is dangerous and leads to failed marriages and children of divorced parents. Hoping that your man will "turn around" once your child has arrived, without addressing his deeper feelings, doesn't usually work. Carolyn and Philip Cowan, in their book *When Partners Become Parents,* found that in couples where the woman went ahead with a pregnancy despite the fact that the man really didn't want a child, they had divorced in all cases before the child reached kindergarten. These couples did not decide ahead of time whether or not to get pregnant. An "accident" happened and nothing was resolved, no feelings were really discussed, no options considered.

Couples who were in agreement and planned a pregnancy, on the other hand, were much more likely to stay together afterward.

However, in between total agreement about having a child and total disagreement lies the vast normal range of ambivalent and even negative feelings that many men have about becoming a father. Your man needs to verbalize these feelings and have you hear and accept them without personalizing them or assuming that his negativity means a definite no. This process can then have a tremendously powerful affect on helping him come to terms with being a father.

This chapter will help you to understand what your man is saying because it is rare that a man says what his real problems are with having children. For example, the statement "I don't picture myself with children" doesn't tell you why this is so or what his feelings are at all. Does the idea make him anxious or angry? Does he think he'll be an inadequate parent or that you'll become a demanding woman? You will find help here in figuring out what he really feels.

Even more confusing to deal with is the man who acts out his feelings through his behavior. In other words, he says yes to children but creates an obstacle through his behavior that makes you decide that you can't have a child with him the way he is. He works all the time and would never take part in caring for a child. Or he's unemployed more than he's employed. The obstacle indicates his resistance and means that ambivalent feelings about becoming an adult and a parent, conflicting feelings, even strong negative feelings exist inside him. In my first book I talked about a man's hieroglyphics. Simply put, hieroglyphics are the pictures on the walls that were left long ago by ancient peoples for us to decipher about their lives, that is, nonverbal messages. These are similar to the pictures that your man paints through his behavior, without words, and they are an indication of what his inner feelings are. Because having a child is such a serious responsibility and is what you may have inwardly hoped for for a long time, now more than ever it is important to pursue what his hieroglyphics mean.

When you finally get your man to tell you his real feelings about having a child, you may be upset. But once you know what they are, you can discuss his objections realistically and possibly resolve the issues. Although upsetting, his negative feelings about having children should alert you to the work that is needed with him but should not discourage you.

There are three types of men who make it painfully difficult for you to decide whether or not to have a child with them. One type is the Obstacle Maker. The second we'll call the I'd Rather Not type. He says he'd rather *not* have a child *but* the decision should be yours. He stops short of an absolute no. The third is called Mr. Noncommittal. He refuses to give you any sign at all or sometimes sounds in favor of having a child, sometimes sounds against it. With any of these men, you will be past child-bearing years if you wait for them to ask you to have their child. Yet it is possible to do what seems impossible: for you to have a child with any of these men and for the three of you to become a real family even though your beginnings were shaky.

There is a man who is usually unworkable—the man who says adamantly no. If you feel you want to try to work on your man who says definitely no, you will absolutely need to be in couples' therapy to resolve the issue. His hard-and-fast stance indicates deeper, more intense feelings that need to be aired with the help of a therapist, not just in the privacy of your home with you as the only listener. Being in couples' therapy will make resolving the conflict easier with any of the men we discuss here.

Let's look at an example of an Obstacle Maker.

Jerry is loyal and committed to Donna, attributes that all women want in their men. He has even said he would consider having a child if Donna wants to. But this has not convinced her to have a child with him. Jerry is far from her dream man because he is at a mediocre-level bank job and has no ambition. She makes more money than he does and would need to work full-time if they had a child. In addition, she would have primary responsibilities at home, as she can tell from living with him during this past year. Jerry also tends to get depressed and mopes around their apartment, which infuriates her.

Donna is torn by indecision; to break up or not, to have a child or not. In her late thirties, she worries that she won't find anyone better. But she can't imagine having a child with Jerry if he won't change. She looks around and sees her friends exhausted and angry from being super working moms. Perhaps having a family is just not for her, she thinks. This thought makes her feel even worse.

Donna loves Jerry but, as Bette Davis said, "Love is not enough. It must be the foundation, the cornerstone, but not the complete structure." Donna has a foundation with Jerry but not a structure in which she feels comfortable raising a child. Someone has to take the lead in building this structure, one composed of two responsible adults trying to do the best for their family. That someone will have to be Donna. Although this seems unfair, we are again forced to adjust to the reality that men like Jerry do not take the first step toward creating the climate for a child. They wait for a woman to motivate or push them. If Donna waits for Jerry *on his own* to become energetic, get a better job, and get help for his moodiness *before* she makes up her mind to have a child or not, she will wait forever. She must jump in and be a catalyst for change.

This chapter will discuss each type of man more closely and suggest what you can do to help him overcome his "resistance" (as therapists describe this) to children. In general, though, men like this don't jump into family life for similar reasons:

1. They feel too insecure about themselves as adults and lack self-confidence.
2. Their own upsetting childhood with destructive parents has left scars that make them afraid to become parents themselves. And if they have children already, unhappy experiences with these children may make them feel anxious about making mistakes again.
3. They are emotionally conflicted, often quite angry, about giving women what they want, especially when that is a child, since a child will tie them to further responsibility. They may not want to share you with a child.

Knowing why he is putting you in this awful position doesn't help you. You think you want to have a child but you can't see this with him (as in the case of Donna and Jerry) because of his obstacles, so you don't tell him what you want. Or you think you want to have a child and need him to be enthusiastic; instead he says it's an awful idea but if you want to, he will. Or you want to have a child and wait for him to agree, but he doesn't say anything. Yet you don't want to leave him; you love him for other attributes he has.

What you have always dreamed of is that the man you love would turn to you and say, "I want to have a child with you." And you then all live happily ever after. But your life is not turning out like that. You may feel incredibly disappointed that this fantasy is not coming true as you had hoped. You see or hear about a man who is eager to have a child and doesn't put up obstacles. Perhaps he even pressures his woman to have a child. You could blame yourself that you didn't find someone who was "easy" like this. But all men are difficult, and your man is the one you love.

TAKING THE LEAD

In your situation right now, you must make up your mind first. You must be the leader and say the definitive words to him: "I want to have a child." Until you do this, any conversation you have with him will go around in circles, yielding no answers. He will not state what he really feels until you have made yourself very clear. But once you've told him that a child is what you want, you can begin to work with a sense of direction and purpose that gets results on the problems he presents. Here is an example of how this worked with Joe, a Mr. Noncommittal.

Andrea and Joe had both been married before, so they were not especially anxious to marry when they moved in together. In fact, they lived together for eight years before they decided to tie the knot. Andrea was ambivalent about having a child but brought up the subject with Joe every once in a while to see his reaction. He would make a joke or say to her, "I don't think you're really serious." Sometimes he seemed interested in the idea of another child to see if he could be a better father this time. (He had a daughter from a previous marriage who was in college.) He never discouraged Andrea from thinking about a child, but he never encouraged her either.

For a while, Andrea made efforts to get Joe to take a stand; she felt she couldn't decide until he made a commitment one way or the other. When that effort proved futile, Andrea turned to herself. Slowly she realized that she would regret not being a mother, not having a child. She made her decision and told Joe.

Joe's reaction was catastrophic. He acted as if she had never before mentioned having children. He was appalled that she wanted to have a child, horrified by her decision after all this time. Andrea was shocked and hurt. She felt tricked. Why hadn't Joe acted this negative before? Now she had made her decision to be a mother, but he didn't want to be the father. She was nearing forty, having spent six years with him. It was unlikely that she would leave him, quickly find another man, and have a child while there was still time.

When the dust around their fighting had settled, Andrea realized that although Joe was horrified he was not saying no. Neither of them really wanted to break up. They went to a marital therapist where Andrea continued to talk about her wish to have a child, and now they discussed Joe's objections more calmly. This was a painful process for Andrea. Much of what Joe said hurt her as he tried to undermine her decision. He wasn't sure that she could really handle being a mother. He said he had never seen her be motherly! Andrea became furious at this and much more of what he said. She had been "mothering" him for years! Other objections seemed insurmountable: he wanted to retire early and relax. How could he do that with a child needing support for the next twenty years?

Yet she found out that he was anxious and worried that their relationship would collapse as his marriage had, and that their child would suffer as his daughter had suffered. He was also, in his negative and backward manner, asking for reassurance that he could be a better father this time.

Andrea's work and stamina paid off. Joe aired all his anxieties and anger about having a child, and within a few months, his feelings had changed. He was ready to have a child.

As you can see, Joe's true worries and objections to having a child could not emerge until Andrea made her own decision. In the same way, Donna will only find out why Jerry is not ambitious, and get him to uncover his own demons when it comes to money and responsibilities and children, if she provides the catalyst. The push that Jerry needs are these words: "I want to have a child with you. We need to work on our money issues and other problems so that we can have a child." For many men, therapy will be the key in working through their conflicts about children and responsibility.

You will need to suggest couples' therapy to begin with, however, as most men will not agree to go for help alone.

MAKING YOUR DECISION

Courage, confidence, and a willingness to take risks are the essential ingredients in getting what you want from the man in your life, including getting him to agree to have a child. But as we have just seen, first you must know what you want. Here are seven questions designed to help you make your own decision. While you think about and answer these questions, you should assess whether these questions make you anxious and why.

DO YOU WANT A CHILD WITH HIM OR NOT?
A QUESTIONNAIRE

1. Will you regret not having a child if you decide, for whatever reasons, not to? Imagine yourself in your later years. Is having a child something you wish you had done in your life?

2. If you decide not to have a child because he's not enthusiastic or he's putting up obstacles, will you resent this forever and perhaps even break up with him eventually?

3. Do you think your life will be enhanced by having a child even if he is not a very enthusiastic father?
4. Will you enjoy having a child even if he is not a very enthusiastic father?
5. If you had a child and your relationship broke up, would you still be glad that you have a child?
6. Having a child is always a risk to any relationship. Is it worth the risk to your relationship to see how it holds up after you have a child?
7. Are you afraid to have a child for your own personal reasons which have nothing to do with him? Could any of these reasons have to do with your own childhood?
8. How much do your career and work pressures influence your decision, as opposed to whether or not he'll be a good or willing father?

Once you have thought about having a child and decided that you want to do this, you are ready to tell him what you want. And you understand that now you have to work on overcoming his obstacles, practical or emotional. Of the couples we looked at, Donna decides to work on having a child with Jerry. Andrea makes the same decision about Joe. These men and yours pose such difficulties when it comes to deciding to have children that we have to look at why you want to have children with them at all. There should be two compelling reasons: One is that you, like Andrea and Donna, love your man. The second is that he has made a commitment to monogamy with you; he wants to be with you. Because of these two compelling facts, you don't want to give him up for someone whose only endearing trait is that he wants to have children.

Yet you feel as if you must be crazy to willingly try to have a child with a difficult man like this. Perhaps you think that even if you do overcome his obstacles, he'll be a bad father. He won't rise to the challenge. But that is not necessarily true. If you overcome his obstacles to having a child beforehand, as we will discuss next, you may be in safer waters than a woman who enters motherhood expecting that her man will be a perfect father. Because there is no such man.

As evidence of this reality, we again look at the research of Carolyn and Philip Cowan. They tell us that even men who very much wanted to have children did less household and child care work than they and their wives had planned when they discussed this before the birth of the child. Men do less and women do more than either expects or wants.

The men did less even though they did not apparently have conflicts about having children. This is because, as Lawrence Kutner of the *New York Times* puts it "New parents discover that, under the unexpected stress and exhaustion of raising a child, their behaviors do not mirror their hopes and expectations." Your man will not be necessarily any worse a father than another guy. But whatever the case, since you know ahead of time the problems your man will present, you will not be deceiving yourself. And you'll be prepared to work on the issues as they develop.

SOME WORDS OF WARNING

Except in a few very special circumstances, there is no right or wrong answer in making a decision whether or not to have a child with a man who puts up obstacles. Tina, for example, decided not to have children because she knew she would have all the responsibilities. Lenny worked late all the time and never did anything around the house. He was an I'd Rather Not type. Tina didn't want to take on the big job of getting him to be a good father since he was so ambivalent. She enjoyed her work as a literary agent and did not regret her decision, although she would have had a child in other circumstances. Margie, however, decided she wanted to have a child even though she had her work cut out for her with her similar man. Having children, she felt, was a necessity for her emotionally.

Neither woman is right or wrong. But there are some "wrong" situations. Should you have a child with David, who smokes marijuana or takes other drugs every day and drinks every night? Even though he's able to hold down a job under these conditions, he is potentially dangerous to a child. Besides the findings about birth defects and low birth weight for infants of parents with drug and alcohol use, he will be unreliable in terms of providing any care for a child since his judgment is constantly impaired through alcohol and drug abuse. You will, in reality, be a single parent with the added burden of this man. If he agrees to go to an AA or NA program or to therapy to conquer his addiction, you can then consider him as a father. Otherwise, pass on having children with this type of difficult man.

The other type of man who is "wrong" as a father is a physically abusive man. You should not stay with a man who is physically abusive to you or have children with him until he has made a commitment to get help and has stopped being physically abusive. He is dangerous until then.

If you are already in a relationship and have a child with a man with either of these problems, you will find help for how to deal with acting-out behavior by fathers in a later chapter.

THE THREE TYPES OF MEN AND THE OBSTACLES THEY CREATE

The man that you love who blocks your way to having a child falls into one of the three types we mentioned earlier: Mr. I'd Rather Not, Mr. Obstacle Maker, and Mr. Noncommittal. We will now examine each type of man more closely to learn exactly how he stops you with his "no" that is not actually a "no."

Mr. I'd Rather Not

This type of man verbalizes every reason you've ever heard for why having children is not for him and why it's a bad idea for you, too. He appears to be extremely sure of his ideas and fixed in his thinking, but he leaves the door open just enough to find a way through it. Unfortunately, you're so angry at him or so tense that you can't see beyond his words and you lose your ability to think clearly. Here is a list of the types of arguments Mr. I'd Rather Not gives you. Once you're familiar with the "lines" he uses, you won't be as shocked and feel frozen in response or get so angry and upset that what you say only further entrenches him in his position.

Mr. I'd Rather Not tells you:

- What do we need kids for? We're fine the way we are.
- I've never liked other people's kids. I probably wouldn't like ours either.
- I like having a good time. Kids tie you down. We won't be able to travel.
- I won't be able to retire early like I wanted to.
- I don't want to give up playing tennis, cards, baseball, etc., for a child.
- I don't think I want the responsibility.
- My family was a terrible place for me. I don't want that to happen again.
- I just hate the whole idea of having children.
- I'm too depressed, tired, or anxious, to have kids.
- I'm not making enough money.
- I don't want to bring children into such a terrible world—and you shouldn't want to either.
- You're trying to get me to become a middle-class boring stiff. You'll just tie me to your apron strings if we have kids.
- I'm afraid I wouldn't be a good father.
- You don't know the first thing about taking care of a child. It will all be up to me.

If some of these reasons sound familiar, it may because you remember Joe, a Mr. Noncommittal. When you pressure a Mr. Noncommittal, he may then turn into a Mr. I'd Rather Not and give you many of these same reasons listed above. This may not seem like progress, but it is. Now you are no longer talking to yourself when you talk about having children. Now he is present to argue with. You can work on his issues and, as we will look at later in this chapter, figure out what his underlying fears are and discuss these.

Now let's look at Nick, who is an I'd Rather Not guy, and his fiancée, Nora. Nick is thirty-seven, Nora is thirty-five. They've been together for five years, engaged for the last year. Nick is an account executive at an advertising agency and is doing well there. Nora is a fashion illustrator. They took nice vacations together twice a year, although they lived separately. Nick got engaged happily enough, but since then Nora has been concerned about the issue of children. For years they had both left the houses of their friends who had children and breathed a sigh of relief. "Thank goodness it's not us." But Nora didn't really take Nick seriously when he said what a pain in the neck children were, or when she saw how uncomfortable he was around kids.

Once they got engaged, she realized that at least one child was a necessity for her. And so she brought the subject up with Nick. Nick said, "My mother told me that you'd want to have children and I'd better figure out whether I'll go along. I really don't like most children that I've met, and they don't seem to like me either. And I like taking vacations. Kids cramp your style. I like thinking I could quit work anytime and just go traveling if I wanted to. Maybe a few years from now I'll feel differently, but I don't know." Nora was upset and sounded so. "What do you mean by at least a few years? I'm thirty-five and can't wait another five years. What if after two years you decide, no, absolutely not? What should I do then? You wouldn't have even talked to me about this if I hadn't brought it up first!"

Nora understandably was angry at Nick, but even more scared than angry. Here she was planning a wedding with a man who wasn't sure if he wanted to have children and leaned heavily toward no. She couldn't sleep and went to a therapy group for help. She saw that she had little idea what Nick's real problems were about children. And that she loved him too much to give up on him. He obviously had deeper reasons for not wanting children; old fears and anger seemed to come out when he talked in such a negative way. Would he be willing to find out about these feelings inside him—enough to eventually become a father?

Although it sounds as if Nick is giving honest and real reasons why children aren't for him, these are only a sign, like a hieroglyphic, of his real conflicts underneath. He is unaware of these conflicts. Let's look at how you can use what he says on the surface to figure out what his deeper and truer reasons really are.

1. Nick mentions that he talked this over with his mother. Knowing his mother, Nora can figure out one of the real problems is his mother, who wants grandchildren so much that she is putting too much pressure on Nick. The only way he can assert himself with her is to defy her by not having children.

2. Nick was always a good and obedient child. From the time he was a toddler, he emotionally took care of his parents, who seemed overwhelmed to him. As a result, he is emotionally depleted. He talks about wanting to take vacations or being able to quit his job, which is really an indication that he wants someone to take care of him because he's tired of putting others first, mainly his parents. He wants to be nurtured. He is completely unaware of these needs. Nora and a child would be more effective in nurturing him and making him feel good about himself than endless vacations would.

3. The other "hieroglyphic" that indicates another deeper issue is when he says that children don't like him and he doesn't like children. No child has ever really said to Nick, "I don't like you." But a childhood trauma did occur which explains his feelings about children. Nick had one older brother who teased him and made his early years miserable. He is unconsciously already making a child into his brother, and he fears that he won't be loved and will even be hated by this child who isn't created yet. He's also afraid he'll lose Nora's love. Once Nora understands this connection, she can re-

assure Nick that what happened with his brother won't happen with their child. She will continue to love him, and so will their child. Having a child could be a very healing experience for Nick.

As you can see, Mr. I'd Rather Not is often not saying what his real feelings about having a child are because he, like most men, does not have self-awareness on a psychological level. His reasons on the surface, however, appear logical enough and he means what he says. But you and he will get stuck if you believe that these superficial explanations he gives are the only story.

Mr. Obstacle Maker

"Mr. Obstacle Maker" is even trickier to deal with than Mr. I'd Rather Not. It's his behavior that is the issue, not what he says. He says yes to having a child, but he lives his life in such a manner that you don't want to have a child with him. Aside from these practical life problems, you love him. Of course at any time you could have a child with him if you decided that you would accept him as he is. (Unless the obstacle is that he won't have sex.) But you don't want to compromise your dream of how you would like a family to be, and you'd like him to at least begin to change before you make such a serious, lifelong commitment as having a child with him. Let's look at the specific kinds of obstacles that Mr. Obstacle Maker creates.

Mr. Obstacle Maker does one or more of the following:

- He doesn't make enough money and is not motivated to make more. He is passive in the way he conducts himself in general.
- He refuses to do anything around the house and doesn't take care of himself too well either. He generally doesn't take care of responsibilities.
- He drinks and smokes too much or gambles so that it interferes in your relationship.

- He works constantly and is not home much now. He would never be home to take care of children or give them quality time.
- He stays out at night with the guys too much. Or he has affairs.
- He is overly involved with his family, so that they control him and try to control you, too.
- He's sick all the time or too tired, so that it interferes with the way he lives or with your relationship.
- He's always pessimistic about life, angry all the time, depressed frequently.
- He doesn't want to have sex or stops when you decide to have a child.
- He's verbally abusive to you and loses control of his anger. (If he is physically abusive, that is an automatic red light to having children unless he gets help.)

Now let's look at Eddie, an Obstacle Maker. Eddie, twenty-nine, and Laura, twenty-eight, got married last year with the understanding that they'd eventually have children. But since they got married, Laura has seen changes in Eddie that make her anxious. His quick temper, which used to be directed at drivers' of other cars or machinery that broke down or the thought of his boss, now comes out full force at Laura instead.

When there was a problem about their checking account the other day he blamed her and broke a door by slamming it so hard. (The mistake turned out to be the bank's, but he never apologized to Laura.) As they drove to her parents' for dinner one night, the car began to make ominous noises. Once again Eddie screamed and cursed at Laura because it was her family they were driving to see. Then last week he began yelling at his boss, too. He was put on warning that he'd be fired if it happened again. Yet when they talk about children, Eddie is definite that he wants some and is pressuring Laura to get pregnant soon. Although she also wants to have a child, she is terrified that Eddie will get fired and is furious at him for the way he is treating her. Once or twice when she really yelled back at him, he stormed out of the house and got drunk, something else he never did before. The man she loved and married has changed so much that half the time she can't recognize him.

Eddie's behavior, not his words, is the obstacle to having a child in this situation. He's jeopardizing his marriage and his job and a potentially wonderful family that he could have with Laura. It is as if he cannot control himself or cannot believe that what he does would stop Laura from being with him. If you ask him, he is definite about wanting to have a family. He loves Laura and can act in a caring way much of the time. But he's "messing up" his life and is unaware of what he's doing or why. Obstacle Makers are best at denying that they have anything to do with the mess they've created around them—until their women tell them loudly and clearly. Laura needs the following help to read Eddie's "hieroglyphics" to know what's going on with him and to determine what to do.

1. When men marry, old family scripts threaten to disrupt the new family. That's what has happened to Eddie. Long-buried tapes from his childhood are emerging as he attempts to build a home with Laura. Despite the fact that his father ran a successful housewares store, Eddie was put in foster care for a few years when his mother was too ill to care for him, even though his father had the money and relatives waiting to provide other alternatives.

Those years were horrible for Eddie and he still feels the effects. He has in fact emotionally moved into another foster home when he moved in with Laura. When he was a child in this awful situation, he felt understandably suspicious and victimized. His anger and frustration about not being able to go back to his real home are coming out in his explosions at Laura. You can especially hear this when he complains about going to *her* parents' house. The fight about the bank account shows his suspiciousness coming out.

2. Eddie has problems with authority figures such as his boss because of his love/hate relationship with his father. He looked up to his father, who then abandoned him by putting him in foster care and later on never helped him in business. Now that he's married to Laura, unconsciously he feels secure enough to "mouth off" to "dad," in this case represented by his boss. But of course his boss has not really harmed him as his father did, and his intense feelings are misplaced and getting him in trouble.

3. Finally, since the message Eddie got was that he shouldn't expect to be treated well or have a successful life, he's following that unconscious message by destroying what he has already built. If he pushes Laura away, he will not threaten the terrible relationship he has with his parents. They will remain the most powerful figures in his emotional life.

As you can see, the fact that Eddie is acting badly toward Laura now that they are married does not mean he has fallen out of love or that she is suddenly a bad person. He is being overwhelmed by unconscious feelings from the past of which he is totally unaware. Were he to become aware of these old feelings, he would no longer need to use Laura or his boss as a target.

Since Eddie is committed to Laura and says he wants to have a child, this indicates the strength of his need for a relationship. Laura will be able to capitalize on this and get him to go with her to couples' therapy to work out his problems with the way he expresses his anger toward her and his boss. Then he can begin to resolve his emotions from the past in a more appropriate way. We will look at how she can do this in the next section.

Mr. Noncommittal

Mr. Noncommittal keeps everything under wraps. What he really feels about having children is up to you to guess. You get very brief comments from him and they're all ambivalent. If you press him to say more, he'll get annoyed but still not give you an answer. These are the types of responses you get from a Mr. Noncommittal:

- He's silent when you say anything at all about children, even other people's.
- He says, "What do you want me to say?" in an annoyed tone when you ask him directly about children. His tone stops you from pursuing this further.
- He says benignly, "Sometimes I can see myself with kids, but then it's such a big responsibility. I just don't know." He looks at you quizzically.
- He laughs or makes jokes when you ask him about children. "Can you just see me bouncing Junior on my knee?" He tells you that the guys at work kid him and say it's a good thing he doesn't have children because he's so . . .
- He says offhandedly, as if you're discussing which movie to see instead of whether or not to have a child, "Whatever you want. It doesn't matter to me the way it does to you."

As we saw previously, lurking beneath the surface of this Noncommittal type may be an I'd Rather Not type once you tell him that you definitely want to have a child. Or Mr. Noncommittal may stay noncommittal. That is what happened with Patrick and Lila.

Lila tried for two years to find out how Patrick felt about having children. As a musician, he was away a lot, but each time he'd return from a tour, she would bring up the subject again. She could never get a definite answer from him. "Sure, honey, whatever you want. You'll be here with the kid more than I will anyway." This was true, he did have to travel for his work. But did he want to be a father or not? "How can I tell if I want a kid? I don't know him yet. I'll see what he's like first and decide if we want to keep him. Ha-ha."

For months Lila argued with Patrick when he made jokes like this. She told him how serious this decision was. How he would have to be involved 50 percent when he was home, especially to make up for the time he was away, and so on. But nothing got Patrick to take her conversation seriously enough to say yes or no. Finally Lila decided she didn't want to wait any longer. "I've decided that I want us to have a child next year. How do you feel about that?" "If that's what you want, honey," Patrick said, barely looking up from the book he was reading. And Lila knew that she could in fact become pregnant. But what kind of father would Patrick make, being so absent emotionally? She was not sure what to do, or how to push him out of his cocoon and into a real conversation.

The Cowans found in their study of couples having children that "one of the most important things that happens in the prebaby period is the way the couple goes about deciding whether to become parents in the first place." The more solidly the couple agree that they both want to have a child, the greater the stability of the family after the child is born. Lila can have a baby, but she rightfully feels that she is making the decision all alone, and that is a risky thing to do. It feels like she's a single parent already. Patrick is not deciding in an involved manner whether or not to have a child. He's walled off his feelings. Let's look at his emotional dynamics:

1. He's terrified of his feelings and so he's acting blasé, leaving the whole decision to Lila.
2. He's scared to take responsibility for such a major decision, so he wants to get her to do it for him.
3. He may in fact be angry about having a child, anxious or scared—we have no idea which it is. We do know that he has feelings because he's so walled off in their conversations. This is a defense.
4. If he's not forced to confront what his real feelings are, he may absent himself more and more after the baby comes, using his work as an excuse.

Lila decides to talk to Patrick in a different way about having a child. She tells him, "I definitely want to have a child but do *you* want to have a child or not?" She refuses to accept his ambivalence and pushing off the decision on her. "When you say it's up to me, that's not an answer. What do you want?" She goes on to say to him, "Once we have a child, it will be as much your responsibility as mine, as much your fault as mine, as much your creation as mine. Getting pregnant will be a decision, not an accident. I think you're scared to say yes or no. If you say yes, then you'll feel anxious about taking on the responsibility. If you say no, you're afraid I'll leave you." Patrick agreed that this was true. He said that he would go with Lila to get help in making the decision.

How to Overcome His Ostacles to Having a Child

The Cowans also found in their study that "when husbands give in reluctantly and resentfully to having a baby in order to preserve the marriage, the child and the marriage may ultimately be at risk." Yet you have a reluctant and possibly a resentful man. Does this mean you should put away thoughts of a child? How do you over-come these obstacles so that if he finally agrees you still have a relationship that is strong enough to withstand the earthquake caused by having a child?

There is a way to overcome his obstacles to having a child so that he does not emerge from the process filled with resentment. First you must accept these three premises:

1. You must be clear you want to have a child and truly believe deep down (although you may have doubts on the surface), that you will both mature and grow as a result of having a child.
2. You must be willing to hear his worst and most unpleasant thoughts and feelings on the subject of children and try not to judge him.
3. You must be willing to suspend any action for several months, if not a year, while you work on the problem.

These are difficult requirements to fulfill and you may feel bur-dened by them. But once you understand these three premises you are in a better position to get what you want from him eventually. Number one is necessary because since he doesn't believe in his own ability to grow to meet the challenge of a child, your belief in him may be the encouragement he needs. Number three is necessary because all change takes time. Working through feelings about having a child is a complex process and requires the space that a year gives. This will not be a wasted year or an easy one because you will be working emotionally all the time. But at the end you very likely will be closer and agreeing on the future. Number two is the crucial point and is the avenue through which he will change. Let's look at this.

BAD FEELINGS DON'T MEAN BAD FATHERS

The expression of unpleasant, nasty, awful feelings can be a cleansing experience. Afterward, the person who has expressed the feelings may feel like loving instead of hating, like nurturing instead of depriving, like being adventurous instead of passive. Bad feelings, in other words, don't mean he'll be a bad father.

But someone has to hear his awful, negative feelings. If he won't go for couples' therapy or elsewhere, you will have to hear him out. That doesn't mean that he should verbally attack you and you sit quietly. What it does mean is that you will need to listen to his doubts, fears, anxieties, and anger about doing what you want—having a child. You will need to accept what he says but point out how things can be different for the two of you.

A few pages back we read about Nick, who recently got engaged to Nora. Here are his arguments against children and the responses that Nora can make:

Nick: I don't like most children I've met and they don't like me.

Nora: Of course you don't like *other* people's children. But it will be different with your own. And children always act as if they don't like adults. They like to be with other kids. Children don't cuddle up to people they don't know. But your own child will love you. I'm sure of that because I love you.

Nick: I like taking vacations and kids cramp your style. This way any time I want to stop working or go traveling I can.

Nora: Kids do cramp your style for a while—but we won't stop taking vacations. We might even have a better time than we do now. _____ take great vacations with their kids. A child doesn't have to take away all our choices—we just have to plan in advance more.

Nora only responds here to what he says. She knows, however, that he has deeper reasons based on his childhood, as we saw several pages back. It is best if a therapist talks to your man about his childhood traumas that stop him from having a child today. Only bring these deeper issues up if he refuses to go for couples' therapy and if your conversations about children are at a stalemate after many months. Then you should make "I think" statements, such as "I think because your brother was mean to you as a child you think our child will be mean, too. And that's not true." Or "I think you're angry at your mother for pushing you to have a child and you're taking it out on me."

As often as possible Nora agrees with Nick, while at the same time showing him that in fact there are alternatives to his way of thinking. She tries hard not to yell, criticize, or put him down, although she wants to do all of these. This is not easy because she is so angry at him, and she wants so much to have a child now, not in five years. After eight months of weekly conversations like these, Nick agrees to have a child but wants at least one year for them to be alone and free together after they're married. Nora can agree to this.

Here's a different example of how to motivate your man to change when his behavior is the problem, not his words. We saw that Eddie became explosive toward Laura and his boss, and started drinking. What does Laura say?

1. I can't have a child with you when you're acting the way you are.
2. I know you're not doing this on purpose and that something's bothering you deep down. You need to talk to someone about your feelings, or we can go together to talk about the problems.
3. You're jeopardizing everything we want.

Since Eddie wants a family, he hears these firm words. He stops exploding at everyone but is still tense. Laura is not convinced the problems are over and a few months later he begins again. This time she threatens to end the relationship unless they go for help, and he agrees.

Only you can decide how much effort you are willing to expend on your man, how long you want to wait for change, whether you want to threaten to leave, whether you want the relationship with him without children. These are difficult questions to answer and you will certainly want to get some help for yourself in answering them if he refuses to change or go with you for help.

Six Steps You Can Take

Briefly then, here are the six possible steps to overcoming the obstacles to having a child that your man presents:

- Encourage your difficult man to express his feelings toward you and about his particular problem (money, family, friends, freedom, etc.) so that he no longer has to act out these feelings.
- Encourage him to express all his feelings about having a child so that he no longer has to act these feelings out.
- Help him to understand how exactly he creates the obstacle to having a child.
- Provide some type of motivation for him to change. Show how it's in his best interest to expand his life, redo the past in a better way with his own child.
- Try to motivate him to get help with you through couples' counseling, individual therapy, or support groups.
- Discuss all the above on a regular basis—in weekly therapy sessions or with him alone in a neutral, unstressful setting, such as a restaurant.

Remember that negative feelings about fathering, about making money, about you, don't mean that positive feelings don't exist also.

They are buried, sometimes quite deeply, under an avalanche of accumulated awful experiences and feelings that need to be dug out so they can live again. Getting rid of negative feelings leads to positive ones.

Unfortunately, your man will not change without your assistance and your ability to see that beyond the conflict that he presents today lies another, more giving and nurturing part to him that has the potential to be a good father. But it is not your fault if he doesn't overcome his resistance to having a child. Never blame yourself for this. You are presenting him with a wonderful opportunity to be more than he thought he could be and to have a more satisfying life than he ever could otherwise. That is your gift to him, whether or not he can accept it.

Eleven Myths about Fathering and What Makes for a Terrific Father

A father who understands what it's like to be a woman and a mother, a father whose vision of motherhood extends beyond the illusion of Madonna-angel oneness, a father who is in touch with the dilemmas of oneness and separateness within himself, is a father who is not afraid to offer his masculine tenderness to his wife and child.

—Dr. Louise J. Kaplan, *Oneness & Separateness: From Infant to Individual*

Whether your man presents obstacles to having a child, or he's excited and joyous at the prospect, having a child and creating a healthy life with a man may be the single most difficult task a woman undertakes in her life. Children are demanding and all-consuming in their needs, and often your man is just as demanding. The writer Dorothy Sayers tells us, "I suppose one oughtn't to marry anybody, unless one's prepared to make him a full-time job." That would make three full-time jobs that a woman could have at the same moment: mother, wife, and career, all of them demanding her full attention. But if men were only different, if they were the father as described by Dr. Kaplan, equally involved in the concrete tasks of parenting, then having a child would not require the monumental work that it does for women.

Two facts in the last ten years point to a crying need to help men to become good fathers and better mates. More women than ever are now working outside the home and having children too. Thus it is imperative and only fair that men get involved on an equal level in parenting.

And second, adult men and women are coming forward and admitting that their fathers fell far short of what they needed. They tell us about their emotional scars which prove that an uninvolved father drastically affects a child. Many of these adult men and women, by the way, had stay-at-home, full-time mothers. Yet they were still damaged by the lack of an involved father. Despite this, today's fathers will continue to parent in the way that they learned from older generations of fathers unless they are taught how to be better fathers and mates—great ones compared to the past. You again will have to show him, even pressure him to change. This is what the next few chapters are about.

We will look at what specifically is a great father, and how he compares to the usual brand of fathers that we have all known. We will explore why men are angry and resentful about having families. Although he loves your child, you feel the impact of his anger and resentment through his lack of cooperation at home and in other problems in your relationship. Thus looking at his anger and resentment is important.

We will explore the emotional issues that prevent men from being great fathers and examine how these emotional issues developed. As always, we will see how you can motivate him to overcome his emotional blocks to being a great father. Last, we will look at how men act out after having children and what women can do to stop this.

First, let's look at what myths society has developed about what it means to be a good father, and compare them to what a real-life great father in the 1990s ought to be.

THE MYTHS ABOUT FATHERING—AND THE QUALITIES OF A REAL-LIFE GREAT FATHER

Society and the family system have agreed for generations not to ruffle the male's feathers. A man is a good father in society's terms as long as he doesn't perpetrate some awful evil (like drunkenness, abandonment, or child abuse). We do not want to upset the male ego and make him feel he needs to do still more. The man who works all day to support his family does enough, the wives of long ago stated. Leave him alone when he comes home. Today's women are beginning to expect more, but our standards for what makes a good father are still far lower than our standards for what makes a good mother. Women become used to filling in the gaps for their man in his relationship to his children.

Here is a comparison between myths that society has used in the past to define a good father, and what a real-life good father needs to be according to today's standards.

ELEVEN MYTHS ABOUT FATHERS AS COMPARED TO THE REAL-LIFE GOOD FATHER

Myth #1: A man is a good father as long as he financially supports his family. (He does not have to be available to his children.)

Real-Life Good Father #1: A truly good father understands that making a living is part of his life and not his whole life. His identity as a father is as important to him as his professional identity.

Myth #2: It's all right for father to be rigid or impatient in the way he plays with children, or not to play with them at all.

Real-Life Good Father #2: A truly good father is flexible and patient, understanding that child-raising requires more flexibility than other situations.

Myth #3: Dads need to have lots of outside interests that don't involve the children: this makes them more interesting fathers (whereas mothers are neglecting their children when they pursue outside interests).

Real-Life Good Father #3: The real-life good father supports his mate to have a career and other interests and be a mother also, just as she supports him to be an involved father and have a career. This support has to be more than verbal. He participates fully at home to free her mentally and physically.

Myth #4: A man is a good father even if he doesn't talk much to his children or to his wife. Wife and child should just "know" that he cares about them. Some men are just the strong, silent type.

Real-Life Good Father #4: A really good father is interested in his wife and child's emotional well-being and in their lives. With words and actions, he forms a strong emotional bond with them.

Myth #5: A man is a good father even if he explodes and loses his temper more often than not (even occasionally hitting). Men are like that.

Real-Life Good Father #5: A really good father examines his own behavior so that he does not express anger through physical force. He admits that he has a problem with anger and works to examine the causes from his past.

Myth #6: A man is a good father even if he talks only about himself when he does talk to his child. He is a good father if he tries to get his children to admire him most of the time but rarely admires their level of accomplishment. They have to perform almost at adult levels before dad will praise them, but after all a dad is supposed to be the keeper of high standards in the family.

Real-Life Good Father #6: A truly good father talks to his children about them and regularly admires even their small accomplishments instead of asking them to improve or seeking to be admired himself. He puts his own ego second when he is with his children.

Myth #7: A man is a good father even if he is critical and judgmental in terms of how he views the world, including his children.

Real-Life Good Father #7: A truly good father controls his tendency to be critical and judgmental, recognizing that this is destructive to his child's growth and to his relationship with his wife. He learns over time to express his criticisms constructively.

Myth #8: A man is a good father even if he frequently yells at his mate and is critical of her, especially if he is kind to his children and doesn't yell at them.

Real-Life Good Father #8: A truly good father understands firsthand the stresses of raising children, and that these stresses are worse for mothers. He is sensitive to this and makes constructive suggestions to his wife, giving her praise as well.

Myth #9: A man is a good father even if he does no concrete work around the house. This means housework and regular care of children. Dads aren't supposed to do those things, yet they're still great dads. If a man does any hands-on child care, he is to be praised to the hilt; a woman is not praised because this is expected of her.

Real-Life Good Father #9: A real-life good father is an equal partner in caring for the house and children, especially if his wife also works outside the home. But he always participates equally when they are home together.

Myth #10: A man is a good father even if he acts out to a controlled extent, having infrequent, brief affairs or is an alcoholic (as long as he keeps his job).

Real-Life Good Father #10: A real-life good father controls his understandable wishes to act out at times. He does not have affairs, drink to excess, take drugs, or gamble destructively. If he is unable to control these tendencies, he seeks help when these are pointed out to him.

Myth #11: A man is a good father even if he does not seek counseling when he needs it. He does not have to have self-awareness or insight. Men just aren't like that.

Real-Life Good Father #11: A truly good father is not opposed to getting help (therapy) and reaches out for it, knowing that his problems will eventually result in problems for his children.

As a result of reading this description, you may feel upset thinking about how different your life might have been if your father had been a really great father like the one described. You are not alone. Few fathers in the past met these criteria.

Without good fathering, we suffer as daughters first, then as single women relating to men, then as wives. Here's Lisa, whose story illustrates what happens without a real-life good father.

Lisa was the middle of three children and had always considered her childhood to be a happy one. The family went on camping trips together each summer. She remembered Christmas trees and Thanksgiving dinners, fireworks on the Fourth of July. Everybody kidded about how tough dad was sometimes. No report card was good enough unless it was all As. If the kids competed, they'd better win or he thought they hadn't tried hard enough. But then dad was a top salesman and said if *he* worked so hard, they should also. Sometimes he ignored them for days if he was really angry or disappointed in them. That hurt, but mom tried to make them feel better.

During college Lisa met Alex and got engaged. After college they married. Lisa knew that Alex had a temper and she often felt criticized by him, but she loved him and that was the way he was. They had a child and Lisa finished her master's degree. She got a good job in business and began to view Alex differently. She realized he was as demanding and critical of their son as he had always been about her. He rarely seemed relaxed. There was always tension at home. Lisa realized that Alex and her father were very much the same. The family joke about dad the tough guy didn't seem funny anymore. She had married a man who treated her the way her father had. Now she felt guilty that her child would grow up with a similarly rigid, critical, and contemptuous father. Her son might even learn to treat women just as badly! Lisa decided that she had to change her lifelong pattern and stand up to the man of the family. Either Alex would change or their relationship would.

Even though Lisa's mom tried to make the children feel better, dad's impact on his children was devastatingly strong. Lisa's father was a "good" father by all the old criteria. But you don't have to look closely to see how destructive he was. And if Lisa had not looked beyond the "father myth," she would have continued to endure her husband's criticisms, tension, and rigidity, believing that was the best a father could be.

Let's look at how another difficult father affected Elana as an adult.

The times Elana spent with her mother on outings were wonderful. She felt special and loved. But Elana had no relationship with her father. He rarely left the house except to work and never accompanied Elana and her mother when they went out. He was silent when he was home; her mother ran the household. Elana never talked or played or had any physical contact with her father except for the few times when he spanked her or yelled at her. Her father did talk to her brother at times about sports events on TV. When Elana questioned why her father was so remote, her mother would tell her not to criticize him: "He's a good father," she said. Elana grew up thinking that it was her fault she could not get her father to pay attention to her.

When Elana began to date, she picked men who treated her badly or left her abruptly. When she finally found Gary, who stayed with her, they married. But he was as passive as her father, unwilling to move ahead at his job, unwilling to go out even to the movies or dinner with her. Playing baseball games or going out with the guys from work was his whole social life.

At first Elana was just glad to have found security with Gary, but she soon felt lonely and isolated. Entering therapy, she realized how furious she was at her father for ignoring her. She felt sad that she had never had a father she could feel close to, who would protect her. She was also angry at her mother for telling her that he was a good father and that this was all she could expect in life from a man. Gary was just like her father and would stay that way unless she acted differently from her mother and said she wanted more.

THE EMPEROR'S NEW CLOTHES

Her mother told Elana that she had a good father and that there must be something wrong with Elana if she wasn't happy with him. Psychoanalyst Jean Baker Miller wrote in 1984, "Western culture has dictated that mothers should uphold the superior importance and the power of the man." This is one of the primary reasons that men have not been asked by their mates to become the truly good fathers that their children and their wives need.

As in the story of the emperor's new clothes in which the emperor's subjects were afraid to tell him that in fact he had on no clothes at all, women have for many reasons refused to admit the truth to their mates and even to themselves. They knew how upset and frustrated they were but ended up blaming themselves instead of blaming the men.

Elana's self-esteem was devastated because her mother and other relatives insisted on upholding the superior importance of her father. And there is another equally bad consequence from upholding the father's importance, when in fact he needs to change. The children, by unconscious habit, get used to having people treat them the way their father treated them: They accept as their fate being ignored and put down, their playful side never developing, their creativity never acknowledged. This pattern will continue throughout the person's life unless other positive, nurturing outlooks intervene.

The myth of what is a good father is really just that—a myth. Just listen to any woman who has children, and you will hear what isn't working in her relationship when it comes to running the family.

What Women Complain about Most

Now that you consider your man as the father of your child, your list of complaints about him may seem worse than before. Are you the only one complaining? Certainly not. To help you realize that you are not alone, we will look at a list of the problems that women encounter most frequently with their men when they consider having a child with him or when they already have a child. When your man says to you that you are a controlling, demanding woman because you ask him to change, remember this list, and all the other women who are experiencing similar difficulties with their men.

1. He doesn't pitch in to do housework at all, or he complains or is nasty or loses energy when it comes to any task related to the house or family.
2. He won't listen to your suggestions or instructions. He has a "better" way to do child-care or housework, which usually results in a problem for you.
3. He doesn't deal with problems directly—whether it's about discipline and structure with your child (he's too tough or too

lenient or ignores the problem altogether), or about relationship issues.

4. He does not, or would not, happily take responsibility for
   children.
5. He works such long hours that all the child-care is left to you.
   When he is home, he has too many important things to take
   care of. He considers your schedule less important than his.
   (There is a small minority of working women who do not have
   this complaint because they are principal wage earners and
   their husbands pitch in more readily to take care of the
   children.)
6. He doesn't acknowledge you now and wouldn't acknowledge
   your superwoman efforts in the future to arrange and take care
   of everything concerning child and family. He takes you for
   granted but wants to be praised lavishly for whatever he does.
7. He's moody. His anger, anxiety, outbursts, or silences control
   the family environment. No one is happy with him around.
8. He's not emotionally supportive or interested in you and your
   feelings. He doesn't know how to be emotionally close to you
   or to his child and resists learning how.
9. Because he acts out his inner conflicts, you can't rely on him.
   (He drinks or does drugs, gambles, has affairs, stays out with
   the guys.)

Although you may not be living with your man right now, you can
still picture a future with him and having children. Then you can
decide whether these problems will be yours based on what you
know about him already. Make sure to address some of the issues
before you take the step to have a child.

WILL MEN BECOME WIMPY IF THEY BECOME MORE LIKE MOTHERS?

In the description of the real-life good father, we described a father who is actually more like what we think of as a good mother. As a result, some may worry that if a man changes to become more like the one described, he will lose his "manliness." Fear about losing their masculine power has been a worry for men for a long time, however. Psychologist Nancy Chodorow believes strongly that men can become more like women in how they parent without loss of masculinity. She says in *The Reproduction of Mothering:*

> Children could be dependent from the outset on people of both genders and establish an individuated sense of self in relation to both. In this way, masculinity would not become tied to denial of dependence and devaluation of women. . . . Equal parenting would not threaten anyone's primary sense of gendered self. . . . Men's primary sense of gendered self may be threatened with things as they are anyway.

Let's follow the story of one man who did change in the direction of becoming a good father, with his wife's help, and didn't lose his masculinity along the way.

Stan already had a grown daughter when he met Susan. He knew she might want to have a child and reluctantly agreed when she said she wanted to become pregnant. But his thoughts of the future were centered more on relaxing than 2 A.M. feedings. Although Stan said he wanted to be a better father this time, he still acted as if their child was Susan's responsibility. She took a few months off from work when Sammy was born and did all the night feedings. Stan tried to get up once or twice but by the time he finally got out of bed, Sammy was screaming so loud that Susan had to calm him down anyway.

Susan knew that Stan didn't handle anxiety well, and there was plenty to make him anxious with a new child. He'd either walk away from the situation or yell a lot. He retreated to his office, leaving her with all the work and decisions.

Once she returned to her job, she started to feel overloaded and angry. She tried just asking him to take on certain tasks, such as calling the pediatrician or giving Sammy a bath. But he'd forget to make the doctor's appointment or turn the bathtime into a nightmare for everyone. Yet Stan evidently loved Sammy and his wife as well. She saw his warm side come out when their life was calm. And so she began a campaign to help him become a good father. She worked on herself to give up some control over what went on with Sammy, and she told Stan that he was doing just what his own father had done. She told him that his yelling was going to make Sammy afraid of him and that he needed help with his feelings of anxiety and anger about fathering.

After a year of talking about these problems, he went for help. Stan has calmed down a lot around their son, and Susan tries to give him ideas about how to spend time with Sammy. Susan tells Stan often how much she appreciates and admires him for his willingness to look at himself so that he can become a truly good father. She notices that he seems to be happier within himself these days. They both realize that overturning old dysfunctional fathering patterns will require time and self-monitoring.

THREE QUICK SUGGESTIONS TO ENCOURAGE GREAT FATHERING

Although the next chapters deal with how to get your man to be a great father, here are a few quick and direct statements of encouragement you can use to propel him in the right direction. Repeat them often to your man in different ways.

1. You will feel better about yourself if you make your relationship with your child and with me as much of a priority in your life as anything else.

2. I will respect you even more as a man if you make us a priority for you.
3. I love you even more and you are even more important to me when you act as a full participant (housework, cooking, child-care) in our home and in the family. I feel hurt when you don't participate.

Some women will feel that it is risky to try to get a man to be a great or even good enough father. "Perhaps he'll leave or hate me!" We know that risk is always involved when you want more in life, but the risk is far less than you think. Your relationship will be fuller and he will respect the efforts you are making, although he may not say it.

Most men, as we have noted, when confronted by a woman who is caring but strong, and definite about the problems he is creating for the child and for her, are deep down grateful that she wants to help him to change for the better.

WHY MEN CARRY AROUND ANGER AND RESENTMENT ABOUT FATHERING

Although some may disagree, even the most loving father has some anger and resentment about having a wife, a child, and financial responsibilities to both. These feelings exist no matter how wonderful his wife and child are. Today's male comedians have found a lucrative way to channel this anger and resentment toward their wives and families when they make fun of them in their comedy routines. Bill Cosby and Rodney Dangerfield are among the most prominent. Since all men feel this way, the feeling ought to be more out in the open for examination and discussion. Instead, however, we make jokes about it or refuse to admit that men resent being family men. But they do.

Men experience anger and resentment to different degrees. The man who abandons his family and never looks back—no support payments, no visitation—is acting out his anger (and other feelings) to a pathological degree. The man who beats his wife and/or children is also expressing pathological anger by acting out. I am not discussing that degree of anger and resentment. It is a far lesser degree that we are going to describe, but it is still anger and resentment—and there is nothing wrong or pathological about the feelings. The feelings cause problems, however, when they are acted upon, denied, repressed, and forced into some other avenue of expression which causes harm to the relationship between the man and his mate or his child.

As we look at the reasons why men have all this resentment about fathering, remember that it's not your job to "fix" his anger or to blame yourself or further put yourself down by deciding that if he was with someone else he'd be happier. He'd feel anger and resentment toward anyone with whom he had a family. The feelings were always there just waiting for the perfect arrangement of wife and child to activate them.

1. A portion of this anger and resentment is derived from the fact that children are demanding and self-centered at various periods in their lives and understandably provoke anger and other feelings in fathers and mothers. Even if he doesn't say he's angry about being awakened at 2 A.M., he may show it in other ways to you.

2. Then there is an unconscious, complex feeling that he has that his wife should somehow be doing better. This derives from the fact that from birth to around age four, and during adolescence especially, children act erratically and irrationally, and perceive the mother (because she is the primary caretaker) as the bad monster who is causing all their internal stresses.

Dr. Helen Singer Kaplan describes what can happen to a man whose own mother let him think that he was always right and she was wrong. Now he sits in contemptuous judgment of his wife during the trying periods with their child:

A nonempathic father finds it perfectly logical to see his wife as a villainess. As anyone can plainly see, the child responds reasonably and perfectly to him and only acts crazy with the mother.

3. Sometimes a man decides that it is his wife's fault because a child is changing his life, even though he said he wanted the child. If your man resents and blames you, his father was probably unhappy and resented his wife, too.

   For example, Calvin is married to Sally. He resents her for tying him down. Calvin heard his father complain frequently that he never got to buy the farm he wanted because he couldn't afford it. Calvin's father blamed Rita, Calvin's mother, who wanted to have children, which kept him glued to a steady job he disliked. And Rita in fact did not support his dream of farming.

   Calvin knows this about his parents. He imitates his father and expresses the desire to do something that Sally hates and that is impractical with two children: living on a sailboat. Then Sally acts like Rita and says no to his dream. In reality, Calvin does not really want to live on a sailboat and he is happy with his job, but the family pattern is to blame the woman.

4. Another reason for the anger that women see or feel from their men after they have a child is jealousy. Jealousy often masquerades as anger and resentment. It is not socially acceptable for a man to admit that he wants more attention from his woman, who undertandably is totally involved with a new baby. He gets angry about totally unrelated and unimportant issues. Jasper is married to Susan. While the baby screams, he keeps right on talking about his day. Susan can't even hear what Jasper is saying. Then Jasper gets angry at Susan for not holding the baby correctly, instead of saying he wants attention. Unfortunately, wanting attention is considered a "childish" feeling. Much anger could be avoided if men would say they were jealous.

5. Still another reason for anger and resentment is that men feel in a second-class role to begin with in the home, and even more so after a child arrives. A man may hate to feel sub-ordinate to his woman, yet he is unable to claim equal power

and time in his family because of society and his own upbringing (you should also assess if you are overly controlling).

6. And last, if your man's mother was bossy, he'll see you as being bossy and think you're controlling him, even if you're not. If his mother was inadequate, he may resent all women because he thinks they want to be taken care of. There are many other ways also that a deficient mother will increase your man's anger and resentment toward you just because you happen to be his mate.

THREE WAYS TO CHALLENGE HIS ANGER AND RESENTMENT

Even though he has social and historic reasons to feel the way he does, you don't want to get blamed for his anger and resentment. Most of the suggestions about how to deal with his feelings and get him to be a great father are in the next chapters, but here are three statements you can use right now to direct his anger away from you and get him thinking about some of the other possible sources of his anger.

If, as a result, he can develop any insight at all into the many other reasons he resents responsibilities and fathering, he will become a much less difficult man.

1. Your anger and resentment don't have much to do with me, and I don't want to get blamed. I'm the person who cares about you the most and does the most for you. You need to get some help because your feelings are overloaded from your past and are damaging our relationship.

2. I feel angry and resentful about all the responsibilities I have around here too, but how is it going to help us to dump this on each other? We have to work together to free each other up from the burdens and learn to give each other praise. (Then ask him to take over a specific job and give him appreciation for this. You will also have to tell him when and how to praise you).

3. Sometimes when you get angry like this I think you're anxious or need my attention but you don't realize it. I'd like you to tell me what you need instead of dumping your anger on me.

Living with someone who acts angry and resentful, and as if he'd rather not be there, is hurtful. So you try to pretend that it's not happening, that he's having a bad day or a bad week or a bad year. Once you understand the universal reasons for his feelings and that this has little to do with you, you will not be as afraid of dealing directly with him using the above statements.

AND WHAT ABOUT YOUR ANGER AND RESENTMENT?

Now it is time to look at your anger and resentment. You probably think that if anyone is going to feel resentful, it ought to be you, not him; he seems to have life so easy compared to you. You have all the burdens of the child and the rest of your life, or you have the job of trying to get him to have a child with you. And now I am suggesting that you add to this the job of getting him to be a great father. With all this pressure, it would be impossible not to feel anger and resentment.

One other feeling we haven't mentioned is disappointment. Women receive a double blow in their romantic lives. First we are fed a rich diet from childhood of romantic literature that builds up the Prince Charming myth as well as the story that fathers are wonderful and know best. Then we become adult women and realize that Prince Charming doesn't really exist and we are carrying emotional scars from childhoods with fathers who certainly didn't know best. Disappointment seems to be preprogrammed into every woman's life when it comes to men and family.

Another reason why women are too angry to see improvements their men make is that they are on emotional overload with work from all their jobs—home and career. And even if he begins to help more in the house or starts to be more cheerful, your work level at this moment is still basically the same. You must then take more time for yourself, even if the house gets dirtier or the laundry is unsorted.

And finally, you may be unable to acknowledge your man's changes because your father mistreated you in similar ways. This produces an overload of feelings that can't be dispelled by getting your present life to improve.

To understand this, let's take Carolyn as an example. Her father was an alcoholic and completely self-absorbed during her childhood. Although he was not violent or outwardly abusive, he ignored her. She yearned to have a relationship with an attentive father and carried severe disappointment and anger about him into her adult life. Now that she is married to Charles, she often has good reason to feel disappointed because he also is self-absorbed and does little to help care for their child.

Carolyn especially needs Charles to help out in the mornings when they are all getting ready to leave. Her daughter has to be dropped off at day care. She finally told Charles how upset she was because he didn't help, and he has begun to make breakfast and dress their daughter. Carolyn has not been able to recognize his efforts. She concentrates on how she is still deprived and how she will be disappointed again, instead of feeling good because Charles is making an effort to change. Her disappointment with her father, who will never improve, is imposing on her present life with Charles, which can get better. Therapy can help her air out the past disappointment and anger and help her get on with her future.

Time for Self-Evaluation

Here is a checklist for you to use to evaluate your own anger and resentment. Honor all your feelings, no matter whether the cause is the past or the present. But get help for them if your past is overloading the present.

1. Think about what your man does or doesn't do that makes you most angry and resentful. Try to recall whether similar

situations happened to you as a child. A history of repeated bad treatment will aggravate your anger toward your man, making you less able to work on the problems now.

2. Do you feel so angry and resentful toward him that you can't stop and acknowledge him when he does or says something positive?

3. Do you often think to yourself, "He'll never make the right kind of father (or mate)," even if he hasn't done anything wrong lately?

4. Do you think to yourself, "He's just like my father. They're all the same," but you're not getting any kind of help to deal with your feelings about your father? (You should be.)

5. If you have a child now, do you identify with your child and think that your child feels toward your man the way you felt toward your own father? (This is not necessarily true. We'll work more on how to separate your feelings from your child's in the next chapters.)

6. When you have a child, it is difficult but necessary to make time for yourself every day. If you don't have a child, you still need to do this. Do you make time for yourself alone every day? If you neglect yourself, every problem he presents will seem worse. (See last chapter for suggestions on how to nurture yourself.)

You have come a long way and deserve much credit for sticking with the relationship that you have right now, whether you have children already or are at the hoping or planning stage. Perhaps you will feel more drawn to the task ahead if you know that the man who becomes a great father will also be a far better mate. Use the eleven traits of a great father as a signpost along with the suggestions in the next chapters, to steer him in the right direction during the time this work will take.

If Glenn is in charge of getting Tania bathed and ready for bed, or dressed to go out, Pat knows that Tania will be crying again. When Tania puts up her usual resistance to her bath or getting her hair washed or getting dressed, Glenn immediately gets into a confrontation, yelling at her before trying to talk at all. He doesn't think he needs to read the books Pat has left around describing how to distract a child from confrontations or why it doesn't pay to "have to be right" with a child.

Tania assumes that she is very bad if daddy is so angry. She must be a bad person. Because these type of incidents are repeated over and over without any change, Tania can grow up depressed, scared of men, and with a negative self-image. Glenn, whose impatience and depression have nothing to do with his daughter, has emotional difficulties that are making him a destructive father although he doesn't want to be. With help and direction from Pat, he could become nurturing.

Sal withdraws, doesn't talk much to his wife, doesn't play with the child. He appears to be silently angry or sad when he's home. Sal did not talk much before he and Sybil had their son, Eddie. Now he is silent except for brief hellos and goodbyes. When Sybil leaves him alone with Eddie, she makes plans for them or gives suggestions about how to play. But when she arrives home, they are always still in front of the TV. Eddie seems bored and quiet watching the TV, not like his usual active, happy self. When Eddie comes to his father with a toy, Sal says he is busy. The more Sybil plays with their son, the more remote Sal becomes. She is glad when he works on weekends because she and Eddie are happier without him around.

Sybil feels lonely in the evenings when Eddie is asleep and Sal doesn't talk much. She's tried to draw him out but he just gets annoyed and tells her nothing is wrong. Eddie meanwhile is becoming a real chatterbox, as long as his dad isn't around, and Sybil finds Eddie is a lot more fun than her husband.

Despite his cheerful appearance, Eddie is feeling the effects of his dad's silences. He will grow up feeling unloved by his father

and try to get his love over and over again. He may not be comfortable in his friendships with men, and he may blame his mother
unconsciously for his father's apparent unhappiness. Sybil could
just ignore her husband and develop a relationship with Eddie. But
it is possible for Sal to get help for his depressed mood if Sybil
strongly works on the problem with him and shows him the negative
impact he is having on her and Eddie.

Peter, Glenn, Sal—three men whose emotional difficulties are causing disruption and potentially chronic unhappiness for their children and their mates. Are they so very different from the average
father? Scenes like these occur in every household once in a while,
but in some households it happens all the time. Regular, frequent
occurrence of this type of neglect, anger, or depression is the criteria for emotionally destructive fathering. (Of course, mothers who
act like this are being emotionally destructive as well.)

All these men love their children, and they can all be better
fathers if they want to be. They can become better fathers if you
want them to be better—and if you are willing to risk conflict in
the relationship for changes that can occur.

Here are more examples of dysfunctional fathering, but this time
we will demonstrate how strong, confident women can turn the emotional tide and change destructive situations into healthy ones.

**Greg volunteers no help and is annoyed when his wife, Lisa,
asks for help. He acts like he can't be bothered to help care
for his child.** Greg has always been hardworking, but since their
daughter Jane was born he's never without a project—fixing doors
that don't close, clipping bushes, and so on. No matter what it is
he's doing, he's annoyed that he's been interrupted when Lisa asks
him to watch their child. Often in front of their daughter he sounds
irritated about having to stop his project to spend time with her.
Lisa is upset that he never volunteers to spend time with Jane (or
cook meals for her or give her a bath), although when he finally
does they always have a great time together. And she's angry that
he acts as if Jane is "her" child and not his also. Lisa feels tired of

dealing with his attitude problem before she can get him to help, so she waits till she is exhausted and feeling impatient and angry before she approaches him.

You can see that Jane could feel that her father doesn't really like her enough to spend time with her, that's she's not very important to him. A message many children get that decreases their self-esteem is that a father's work is more important to him than his child. Jane could also internalize the message that work in general is more important than relationships. Everyone has work that takes them away from their children, but Greg is using his work to run away from his family due to unconscious feelings about fathering. With confidence, Lisa can:

- explain to Greg that although he loves his daughter, his annoyance can make Jane feel unwanted by him. He must hide this annoyance from her and give Jane more time in his day.
- tell him that either he should go alone for help or she will go with him to talk about how they feel about parenting.
- tell him that she thinks there are issues from his past interfering with his ability to be an attentive father today.

John scares his child, intimidates him, bullies him, and has to be right. John insists he knows just what their son needs, and it's not to be pampered and spoiled by his wife, Joan. But when he's with five-year-old Sammy, the boy ends up crying. When they roughhouse, John jumps at Sammy as if he's an adult wrestler. When they play ball, John tells him he acts wimpy. When they play games, John acts as if he's the child and has to win all the time. He pushed him into deep water last summer, and Sammy became terrified and now won't go in at all. John talks in front of Sammy about his own parents' illnesses, which have been especially gruesome, and mentions all kinds of tragedies that he hears about at work. Sammy is becoming a fearful child, which is alienating him from his father even more.

Sammy also feels that he can't do anything right and that he's not acceptable to his father the way he is. Of course he's scared of his father. Joan is withdrawing from John more and more, too. She's angry at him but is scared to confront him. Joan needs to:

- go for help herself to build her confidence to deal with John. Joan is making John seem too powerful because she was scared of her own father as a child.
- tell John that he's making Sammy into the very type of child he dislikes—a fearful child. She also needs to say that John has to help Sammy feel secure and confident—and that John can learn how to do this.
- tell him that Sammy is a "real boy" even if he's not as tough right now as his father.

Marty is critical of the way Marion takes care of their child and never acknowledges how tiring it is to care for a child. He blames her every time things don't work out right. He never says that he appreciates the work she does. Marty acts as if taking care of a child is a breeze. He looks at Marion as if there's something wrong with her when she complains about all the work or about losing sleep at night when their son, Eric, has a bad night. He tells Marion that his mother raised three children without any help and never complained; that if you ask her to this day, his mother says how much she loved raising her kids. Marty also thinks Marion should be able to control their very active son better, that their son should be better able to dress himself and eat quietly. He thinks that she's generally not as good a mother as others.

Whenever Eric is upset and cries, Marty blames Marion. When Eric is overtired and cranky on the way home from an outing to the zoo, it's Marion's fault for not planning the day better. If Eric bumps his head coming out from under the table where he's been pretending to be a dog, Marion shouldn't have let him do this and it's her fault. Marty, of course, was there for the whole series of events, too.

Marty criticizes and blames Marion in front of Eric. Eric may grow up with as little respect for his mother and other women as his father seems to have. Marion feels more crushed and defeated each day. She has fantasies of leaving Marty but doesn't tell him how angry she is and doesn't forbid him to attack her with his pointless and untrue criticisms. Here's what Marion can do:

- Walk away from Marty when he criticizes her in front of the child.
- Tell him when they are alone that he attacks her and she won't stand for it.
- Get help for herself—a support group or individual therapy.
- Tell Marty that he needs help: he is overly anxious and angry because of his family history. He is confusing her with his mother and father. His intense moods are going to destroy their relationship and cause their son to have problems.

Robert mopes when attention is not on him, stops the fun when Karen is laughing with their child, tries to get praise for himself and withholds praise from the child. Robert was an only child, and Karen thinks that's why he's moped around the house since the day that Cheryl was born. He's just not used to sharing the attention. Karen is thrilled to have a daughter and plays with her all the time. But she's aware that Robert never joins in. This is a real different side to his personality. He'll be the life of the party if the attention is on him. Robert does help with child care. He diapered Cheryl when she was small and helped to feed her. Now he only pays attention to her if she's laughing and smiling at him. When she cries, he leaves the room.

Karen sees how hard Cheryl is already trying at the age of three to keep him happy. If they are drawing together or playing a game, Cheryl will tell her father what a nice drawing he made. She tells her mother that daddy wins at games they play, but that's all right because he's a bad loser. Karen feels like Robert needs constant praise. But Karen is busy and can't always provide this. She's also getting annoyed about having to emotionally feed two children. What about her?

The little girl has already figured out how to make daddy feel good and has low expectations for how she should be treated. She may grow up to be a "caretaker." Karen is confused about what to do. She feels too angry and tired to nurture Robert so that he can be a better father. Karen will feel better after she:

- tells Robert they must go together for counseling. They are both feeling depleted and need help.
- explains to Robert that he must praise Cheryl and make Cheryl feel good about herself when he is with her. She could grow up with a bad self-image otherwise.
- asks him to spend specific weekend time doing a particular activity with Cheryl.

You can feel the power of these type of interventions and how effective, over time, these women can be with their difficult men. The women are direct, caring, confident, and firm about what is wrong and what changes are needed. They are not attacking the men or blaming them, and they do not expect overnight miraculous changes. All the women, however, recognize that they, too, will need help in order to deal with their mate's problems constructively.

You will know better how to communicate with your man if you understand that there are submerged feelings causing him to act badly and propelling him to be impatient, withdrawn, angry, self-centered. Habits learned from his family also cause him to act inappropriately as a father. But right now we will look at the feelings that are being pushed away. Your man most likely doesn't know he has these deeper emotions, or he won't admit he has emotions that appear to him so "feminine." Let's see what these hidden feelings are.

THE DEEPER FEELINGS THAT CAUSE HIS PROBLEMS

We read about Marty, who blames Marion for every small or large conflict that occurs with their son. Why is he like this when another man would be understanding and supportive? I explained to Marion that Marty criticizes himself as harshly as he criticizes her. Yet Marion said to me this couldn't be true. She had never heard him blame himself for anything. If anything, she said, he tried to pass the buck to someone else all the time.

Yes, on the surface, Marty lets himself off the hook and puts Marion down. But look at the world from what has to be Marty's point of view. Every big or little mishap in life has to be blamed on someone. Nothing can just be a mistake or bad luck or something that could happen to anybody. Marty has what is known as a "severe superego," to use psychological terms. Judgments are part of his makeup: he is never free of them. Deep down he is either judging himself every minute or trying to blame others. He is tormented by this way of looking at life, as tormented as he makes Marion feel. He feels anxious and inadequate all the time.

That is why Marty acts the way he does. And it takes this kind of real detective work to figure out Marty or any man. He makes it hard for you to understand him. He makes it hard for you to love him. He can't even understand himself. That doesn't mean, however, that you should endure his problem forever.

Gloria Steinem was talking about family life and relationships when she said, "The first problem for all of us, men and women, is not to learn, but to unlearn." The seven men we looked at need to unlearn the bad emotional lessons taught to them at home and by society. Society teaches men not to let anxiety, sadness, and tears show.

Men also learn the disastrous lesson at home that any feelings that make you vulnerable, not strong, are bad and must be pushed aside. When these vulnerable feelings are denied, other worse feelings and actions take their place to cover them up. Here are the primary, unconscious vulnerable feelings that your man is avoiding and that cause him to be emotionally destructive as a father:

JEALOUSY

Jealousy is a perfectly normal feeling for your man to experience when you have a child, especially in the beginning when you are spending so much time and concentrated effort on your baby. You have been two, now you are three. He has to share you, give you up for a while, and he doesn't want to. Parents rarely have more than thirty seconds to hold a conversation when a child is awake, but your man still wants your attention and care.

All of the men we read about are feeling jealous. Jealousy is one of the underlying reasons why they act the way they do. The man who can say, "I'm jealous of how much you love our child" or "Do you still love me now that you love the baby so much?" is a man who will have less need to withdraw or mope or become angry to cover up his jealous feelings. When he is more difficult during and after pregnancy, jealousy is present.

Robert, who tries to get his daughter Jane to praise him and mopes if attention is not on him, is an especially jealous man. His family played favorites when he was a child, making one seem special while ignoring the others, and comparing them to each other. When his parents ignored him, he felt as if he didn't exist; when they praised him he felt like a superstar. He was furiously jealous of his sister and brother whenever the attention was on them. Robert needs to develop some awareness that he is transferring the feelings from the past onto the present with his daughter.

INADEQUACY AND USELESSNESS

Children at any age can make a parent feel inadequate, especially a new parent who is facing each situation for the first time and experiencing normal confusion. Feeling inadequate gives rise to feeling helpless. Helpless, inadequate, useless—no words could be further from society's description of a real man. Yet that is how most fathers (and mothers) feel much of the time. Your man then receives a second dose of inadequate and useless feelings because, according to the culture, you are supposed to be "in charge" of the child raising. He starts off feeling like the junior partner in the family firm. Since feelings of inadequacy are totally unacceptable to all men, you will not hear your man admit he feels this way. He can barely admit how he feels to himself.

Marty feels inadequate as a father, but since he can't admit this, he tries to make Marion feel as inadequate as he feels. John has always been unsure of himself. Fatherhood has only made him worse. He covers up his feelings of inadequacy by bullying his son. You can see all the serious conflicts that can result from this double dose of inadequacy. Here is a specific example of what happened to another couple, Diane and Zach, when Zach felt helpless and covered it up.

It is the middle of the night. Diane and Zach hear a noise that sounds like a seal's bark come from their one-year-old son's room. They have never heard anything like it before, but they have read that this noise means he has croup. They run into his room and see he is gasping for breath. Both of them are scared, but Diane remembers that steam helps and she tell Zach to turn on the shower in the bathroom to create steam. He tells her that she's panicking and she should just calm down. Diane goes and does it herself. Diane then goes to call the doctor, and Zach tries to stop her by saying that she's making this worse by getting hysterical. Diane doubts herself for a minute, then realizes she is not hysterical but now is furious at Zach. She makes the phone call. Diane takes the baby into the bathroom and after a few minutes in the steam the attack passes and he is breathing normally. The doctor returns the call and Diane speaks. He reassures her that she has done the right thing and gives her advice about the next time this occurs.

Diane and Zach's child has survived the croup, but their relationship is in trouble because Zach felt helpless and inadequate and scared but couldn't admit this to himself. Instead, he tried to make Diane feel as he felt. Diane did feel all of this but was aware of it and could then move on to deal with the situation. Diane said she would much prefer if he showed and accepted his helplessness. If he ran in circles it would be more helpful than trying to make her feel worse. Zach criticizes Diane when she is trying to cope constructively with a frightening situation. Consequently, Diane feels furious and alone, knowing that the next time a crisis occurs, Zach will not help her. She will have to feel helpless yet handle the crisis alone and be criticized at the same time.

A man's unconscious mind will go to great lengths to avoid consciously feeling inadequate and useless. This is because the feelings are so intolerable to him. To get rid of these feelings, he criticizes and tries to make you feel the way he really feels inside. If he can get you to feel as inadequate and useless as he does, then he will feel better. Your man does not do this on purpose, but it is destructive all the same. We will see what you can do about this in the next section.

DEPRESSED, SAD

There are many reasons for a father to feel depressed and sad when he has a child. Since having a child emotionally makes us think about our own childhood whether we want to or not, the result can be that your man feels depressed if his past was not happy. Another reason that he could feel depressed is that a child is a reminder to your man of his own mortality. And still another reason for sadness is that your man may mourn his youth and his freedom to come and go as he used to.

Unless he is in therapy, however, it's unlikely he will be aware that he feels depressed for any of these reasons. Instead, he will act the way the men we previously described acted—angry, frustrated, even critical, or perhaps silent and withdrawn. Glenn, who was impatient and angry with his daughter, feels sad and depressed and empty inside. He feels like *being* taken care of, not taking care of another person. His impatience and anger show that his nurturing supplies are low.

We looked earlier at Sal, who was withdrawn and silent watching TV for most of the time that he spent with his son. Deep down, Sal feels depressed and empty. No one paid much attention to him as he was growing up. His parents worked all the time. He received little nurturance, little praise; no one talked much and everyone seemed unhappy. He goes through life feeling deprived and thus depressed because of the attention and nurturance he never received. When he is with his son, he withdraws because he can't give what he never got. The more he watches Sybil play with their son, the sadder he feels unconsciously, realizing what he missed. Deep down he also feels jealous of the kind of mothering he never had.

Sal and Glenn need the help of a support group or counseling with a nurturing therapist to help their depression and fill some of those empty places inside. They'll then have more emotional energy and see an example of how to be giving to another person.

ANXIETY AND FEAR

Taking on the responsibility of raising a child is a scary business. Children break legs, break windows, get in and out of trouble as easily as you get in and out of bed. And even when they don't cause trouble, life can be dangerous anyway. Fathers and mothers must know that anxiety and fear will be their companions once they have a child. Yet as usual many men refuse to acknowledge their appropriate anxiety and show it instead in destructive ways.

Marty, who criticizes his wife, is really very anxious. When he's with his son, he's afraid that he will be blamed if something goes wrong, if Eric falls or cries. This is what happened to him as a child. He was told to take care of younger siblings who of course were always in trouble or having accidents. Then he was blamed when anything happened. He's become overprotective and critical to alleviate his anxiety. Meanwhile, Sal, the withdrawn father, is also anxious deep down. He came from a family of worriers who expected the worst to happen all the time. To cover up his overwhelming anxiety, Sal becomes paralyzed and withdraws. Both of these men have normal anxiety plus an added dose because of their family backgrounds.

Author Alma Routsong wrote, "I wonder if what makes men walk lordlike and speak so masterfully is having the love of women." If your love and attention do in fact make your man feel like the lord of the castle, then losing that love and attention, even in small part to a child, can cause anxiety. Suddenly he no longer feels needed and wanted. You still admire him but don't have time to show it anymore. You're using up your store of praise for your child, who demands it or needs it more. As you now know, he will get angry or withdraw or mope in order to get your attention—instead of telling you that he feels scared and anxious that he has lost you.

Men may also feel afraid that their own children won't love or respect or admire them. Again this will be more likely to happen if they were not loved as a child by a parent or sibling. John, who bullied his son and always had to be right, is actually quite fearful underneath all his blustering. He's afraid that his wife and son don't really want him or need him around. He is particularly afraid of this because his brother and father acted like they didn't want him around at times. Group or individual counseling and reassurance that they are not at fault and are good parents will help these men be better fathers.

ANGER

Finally we come to hidden anger. You won't recognize this anger because it is not expressed in any form that is recognizable. This hidden anger is often responsible for why he is hard to live with and not the father you hoped he would be. When Robert mopes, he is also unconsciously angry. When Greg is never there to help with their child because he has an important project to finish, he is also angry. When Sal sits and watches TV, he may be feeling angry underneath. When Glenn is angry about spilled juice, it's not only about spilled juice.

All these men feel the anger we have discussed before, anger about being responsible for another person; anger about not being the center of attention; anger about not being able to do what they want to do when they want to do it because their child comes first. Then there is also anger because their own parents never took care of them as well as their child is being taken care of now. This anger is not restricted only to fathers, and you can surely identify with these feelings.

MORE ON HIS FAMILY INFLUENCES

Family history is once again responsible for your man's most intense unconscious feelings. Even though it looks as if the "here and now" (you and your child) are the only reason that he is so upset in one way or another all the time, his family upbringing is the primary reason that these feelings are getting too unwieldy and causing everyone too much misery. From reading chapter four, you know how important his family influence is. Once he has a child with you, the unconscious influence of his family on him quadruples. (Your family's unconscious influence starts to affect you more as well, so remember to always work on your own self-awareness while you're thinking about his.)

To summarize, here are the three most important ways that his family history affects him and thus distorts and damages his relationship with you and with your child:

1. Specific upsetting, traumatic experiences from his past influence him in the present unconsciously. When a similar situation occurs with your child, it triggers an inappropriate response from him as a father because the situation is ringing an unconscious bell in his memory.
2. He sees you unconsciously even more as if you are his mother or father, assumes that you are as incompetent as they were, as anxious, as controlling, as mean, as unloving and uncaring, as closed-minded. He may unknowingly try to get you to act toward your own child or toward him as his parents did. He

may not want to have a different kind of life than his parents had.

3. You see him change before your eyes from the man you loved to a man who is much like his father or mother in negative ways. He then proceeds to act toward his child and toward you the way his parents acted toward him and toward each other. When he acts this way, he is very different from the man you love. He is either unaware that he is acting like them or thinks it's perfectly okay.

But change is possible, even for your difficult man. Let's see how.

How to Get an Emotionally Difficult Man to Be a Great Father

As a parent, you feel like you are the mother in the middle, caught on one side by your love for your child, on the other by your need to have a good relationship with your man. You often feel torn apart. If you go along or ignore what your man is doing or not doing right as a father, than you may be hurting your child. But if you argue with your man to get him to be a better father, a rift forms between you and him.

As upset as you feel, you know that if you don't now deal with his emotional issues that make him a destructive father, you may instead have to deal with the results later on in problems with your child. Once again, he will not change unless your push him to. Of course, you always need to be examining your own emotional issues and how they may be negatively affecting your child.

What to Expect When You Talk to Your Man

You must begin by accepting that no matter how much you try to figure out the best way to talk to him, you will step on his toes. He will not be happy when you begin to talk about the problems you have with him as a father. He will probably be angry. That is the primary emotional risk you will take. It is very unlikely that he will leave you. Life with him may be more unpleasant for a while because you have brought up these issues. But this will pass.

Other than talking about sex, there is no topic more sensitive than a person's ability as a parent. So to begin, always let your man know that you hate to hear about your mistakes also, but that you want him to tell you what he doesn't like as well.

When his parenting skills are being critiqued, he will feel guilty that he has made mistakes with his child, angry because he thinks you are wrong, anxious that perhaps you are right. He will deep down feel like he is a bad person if he has not been "right" as a parent. He will fight back in whatever is his usual style.

If he is a verbally aggressive man, he will tell you that you are worse than he is. If he is a withdrawn type, he will say nothing, so you will not know what he is feeling. Ideally, of course, he will think about what you say and agree to work on the problem.

But even if he says you are completely wrong, do not despair. He has heard what you feel and his unconscious mind will now wrestle with the problem you've presented. You will have to discuss this many times. Weekly reminders and monthly discussions, to let him know that the issue is still there. Be wary, however, of becoming an "overcomplainer" described in *How to Love a Difficult Man.* Don't yell every day at him or endlessly discuss the problem.

GOALS FOR YOUR DISCUSSION

First, let's define a discussion. A discussion is not screaming at him furiously when you are fed up or angrily confronting him. What is a discussion? It is defined as having a talk with him about what you feel and want and hearing what he feels and wants. You may have specific goals in mind but they may not be achieved in the discussion.

Know what your goals are before you have any discussion. Your goals are twofold. Your short-term goal is to ask him to change his immediate behavior. This means, for example, that you want him to

- stop yelling so much at bathtime.
- start playing and talking with his child more in the evening.
- stop criticizing you or your child.
- take over child care at a particular time without seeming annoyed.
- to praise your child more and not bully him.

Your long-term goal is to help him become aware that he has unconscious feelings that are making him emotionally destructive and to motivate him to find out more about these feelings on his own. Don't try to tell him exactly what he feels unconsciously if he reacts negatively to this, however.

You also want to create a mutual support system around parenting issues and to create a climate for discussions and expression of feelings when either of you is upset. You will have a much better chance of accomplishing your goals if you are not only talking at home but are also in couples' therapy. Getting him to go with you for therapy is another long-term goal.

GUIDELINES FOR DISCUSSIONS

1. Never have any lengthy conversation about his parenting problems in front of your child.
2. Be *specific* about the problem. Bring up one problem only at a time.
3. Do not bring in everything he does or has ever done that is wrong. Watch out for "always" and "never," as in "You always do this wrong; you never do anything right."
4. Always mention positives and praise him at the same time. There are *always* positives you can talk about. For example, he did go along with having this child so that now you have a child you both love.

5. Be understanding about how hard it is to be a parent, about the pressures you are both under.
6. Be understanding about how hard it is to be better parents than your own parents were. (But be clear that is your goal.)
7. Include yourself. Say that you are also making mistakes because you don't know any better, because of your own upbringing, and that you feel frustrated, like withdrawing or getting angry. You feel as he feels.
8. Be clear that you want change to occur.
9. Tell him specifically what he can say or do differently in the situation you have just described to him.
10. Make concrete suggestions as often as possible if he is able to hear and use the suggestions—about how to talk to your child, how to spend time, how to distract from confrontations, how to set limits.
11. Remember that change will not be immediate.

WHAT TO SAY TO YOUR CHILD

Since we know that difficult men do not change overnight but children are affected on a daily basis by negative parenting, you can take immediate steps to minimize and defuse the effects of his interaction or lack of such with his child. Here's what you can do:

1. Tell your child clearly that it is not her fault that daddy is yelling too much or ignoring her or being critical.
2. Explain that daddy is upset about other things and/or is "in a bad mood."
3. Be clear that daddy should not act this way with her (or him). Do not say that daddy is a bad or terrible person but that the way he talks or acts is wrong.
4. As your child becomes more verbal, encourage your child to tell daddy directly what she (or he) thinks and feels when daddy does not treat her as he should. Teach her to express

her feelings appropriately and without attacking. (Do not allow your child to do this if your man becomes abusive toward the child in any way because of what he or she says.)

5. Encourage your child to tell you also what she feels toward you if she is angry or upset (expressed appropriately and not as an attack).

In the *Second Shift*, Arlene Hochschild says, "If women lived in a culture that presumed active fatherhood, they wouldn't need to devise personal strategies to bring it about." Despite everyone's best enlightened and liberated intentions, you still need to devise a personal strategy to get your man to take an active role in the family. The guidelines just given (and those in the following chapter) will help you do that.

But these guidelines should accomplish more than his watching the child on a Sunday morning. We want fathers who are nurturing and patient, who communicate verbally, who express their feelings and accept the feelings of their children (and mate). We want the emotionally great father. Often when you struggle to help your man grow emotionally, you will feel alone. But you are never really alone with this problem. All women in one way or the other meet up with the emotionally lacking father. But it is the courageous woman who attempts to change history by working with her man to create a father who is not only as active in child care as she is, but who embodies the best emotional traits of a good mother as well.

EIGHT

When Fatherhood Makes Him Act Out and What You Can Do

When you prevent me from doing anything I want to do, that is persecution; but when I prevent you from doing anything you want to do, that is law, order and morals.

—GEORGE BERNARD SHAW

A 1984 study found that "men's moods and behavior tend to affect the quality of the marriage more than women's moods and behavior do." Although this doesn't sound fair, it is the reality. If your man acts destructively, the emotional stability of the family is even more at stake. We've studied his moods; now let's examine his behavior after becoming a father. Here's an example of what it means to "act out" after a child is born.

George was the picture of the perfect husband during Rita's pregnancy. He came home early from the office at night, went with her to natural childbirth classes, was sympathetic to her complaints, and did more housework than usual. Yet as soon as they brought their daughter home from the hospital, George disappeared into his office. He took on more assignments at work, left early in the morning, stayed late every night, worked often on weekends. Rita complained to him of loneliness and feeling angry about being alone with the baby all the time, but he did not respond. Then Rita realized that more than work might be keeping him away. She began to check up on him at work and found out that he had been having dinner with his secretary more than working. When she confronted him, he said it was just a friendship. He needed someone to talk to because Rita was so preoccupied with the baby all the time. Rita was outraged. The baby was not just some hobby she could give up. This was their child and George sounded as if the baby didn't matter to him.

Whether George was actually having an affair or a serious flirtation, the psychological term for his behavior is "acting-out." Acting-out can be defined as expressing unconscious, repressed feelings through actions, actions that are usually destructive to one-self or one's relationships. Therapists understand that the more an individual is aware, can recognize and acknowledge these repressed feelings, the less the individual will need to act out. We use this theory when we work with individuals who act out. You can do the same with your man.

George had never acted this way before, but the addition of a baby to his life caused immense, deep psychological upheavals for him. Unfortunately, he was completely unaware of this and the only form he unconsciously found in which to express the festering feelings inside was through acting-out.

You might compare George to a volcano. Inside a volcano, steam builds up, and the greater the pressure the greater the likelihood of an explosion. Inside George, or any man who acts out, are stored-up feelings. As the feelings increase, so does the pressure and the likelihood of an explosion expressed through acting-out behavior. Whether we talk about men or volcanoes, explosions cause destruc-tion. Scientists can predict volcanic explosions with greater accu-racy these days and save lives. Unfortunately, it's not as easy to predict when a man will act out because we can't measure his stored-up feelings. You do, however, know your man and know whether he holds everything in. And you can venture a guess as to how strong his emotional conflicts will be about having a child if you examine his original family. So you don't have to be completely in the dark about when or if he may act out.

TEN WAYS THAT MEN ACT OUT AFTER YOU HAVE A CHILD

Here's a list of the ways he upsets you, from the mildest forms of acting-out to the most severe, after you have a child together. Ac-tions often do speak louder than words, and all these behaviors should grab your attention because something is going on underneath. We'll look at what you can or cannot do to help him change these behaviors next.

1. He repeatedly messes up the caretaking of your child when it's his turn, despite instructions and discussions.
2. He takes on new interests, hobbies, courses, projects that take up so much of his time that they preclude his being with you and your child.
3. He refuses or makes no attempt to get a better-paying job even though he could and money is needed.
4. He loses his job or causes problems at work that threaten his job.
5. He becomes a workaholic or is always out with the guys, never spending time at home or with you and your child.
6. He gets sick more often, has accidents, gets himself into trouble legally, or loses things all the time.
7. There are changes in your sex life. He does not want to have sex or pressures you to have sex when you don't want to.
8. He has an affair or serious flirtation.
9. He suddenly drinks to excess or takes drugs.
10. He becomes physically aggressive, even·violent, with you or the child.

When your mate acts in any of these ways, you are the only one who wants to know what is going on underneath for him. He doesn't want to know. He's too busy acting-out to be self-reflective. As the neglected wife in the movie *Moonstruck*, Olympia Dukakis pondered this question: Why was her husband suddenly, after thirty years of marriage, having an affair? Her husband was caught up in acting-out and had no idea why he was behaving this way. She asked several men for their opinion and thought of an answer herself: to avoid thinking of death. The explanation felt right to her. Once she understood, she confronted him and the affair stopped.

This story is of course simplified for the movies, and the husband had other unconscious reasons for having an affair at that time ("empty nest" anxiety about his daughter's impending marriage, for example). But what Ms. Dukakis did illustrates two important points: She did not blame herself so that she became paralyzed with insecurity. And she faced the problem with a strong, firm idea of what she wanted. This is what you also will need to do in order to stop your man from acting-out. The Tough but Tender Talk approach follows, which will help you to be clear and confident so that you can get what you want from him, even if you feel insecure and at fault.

A better resolution to the problem Ms. Dukakis had in *Moonstruck* would have included couples' therapy. Using couples' therapy, she and her husband could have learned if any problems in the relationship and in their individual histories might also have led him to have an affair. In other words, if changes in the relationship might make them both happier. However, even if Ms. Dukakis's movie husband were unhappy with her in the relationship, he owed it to himself and to his wife to *talk* about the changes he needed, not act out instead. Acting-out is *never* the appropriate or constructive measure to take. Acting-out causes more problems and solves nothing.

A very serious form of acting-out that has become an epidemic is observed in those men who do not see their children after divorce or who disappear and do not pay child support. Discussing this very serious problem requires more space than we have here. We will look at men who stay in the home but who take actions that are destructive to the family.

DON'T BLAME YOURSELF!

It's always too easy to find fault in yourself if he's acting-out, and this is even more true after you have a child. You're heavier than you were before because of childbearing, and you don't have time yet to "look good"; he's staying away from the house more. You assume that the reason is your weight instead of recognizing the deeper emotional issues that occur for him now that he's a father. He's at work, or into a hobby, a new project, or worse still, an affair. Or he's just not as interested in sex as he used to be. You aren't either, but you still want to know that he wants you. You feel abandoned physically and emotionally, and you feel your self-confidence eroding.

Don't attack yourself. A man's acting-out behavior is primarily caused by deeper, more intense feelings that have little to do with you. Feelings multiply and intensify when you have a child, as we have seen in the previous chapter. If he was not a psychologically aware man to begin with and now his feelings are growing, they will have to come out in some form. Acting-out behavior is one form they can take.

Blaming yourself never helps. You can, however, at the end of this chapter, evaluate yourself objectively as to how you may be unknowingly contributing to his negative feelings about having a child—for example, by controlling the childcare situation too tightly or by ignoring him when he's home. We will discuss here how you can improve.

The woman who has to deal with an emotionally difficult man feels upset but may not be able to describe exactly what he is doing that makes her feel so badly. Acting-out is easier to see, easier to pin down. It is a concrete action you can describe that you do not like, as opposed to emotional abuse that you have trouble recognizing. We will look at the ways he acts that upset you, why he does this, when you should do something about it, and when you should detach.

THE DEGREES OF ACTING-OUT

Acting-out can cause anything from mild ruffles to vast, turbulent catastrophes. But behavior is the bottom line. If he *says* awful things but his behavior is consistently caring, you're confused but feel loved anyway. But when he *acts* badly after promising you great love, you feel betrayed and that his words mean nothing at all.

There are, however, a few situations where the acting-out behavior doesn't really bother anyone and can even be helpful in the short run. For example, Jane preferred to spend uncomplicated time with her child rather than worry about Ralph's moods. Ralph acted out his feelings of rejection. He decided to become a chess wiz and he was not home as much. He spent Saturdays and evenings playing chess. Jane found this to be a relief, especially since she had built a network of friends who had children, and she spent pleasant time with them.

But in the following situation, when the man acted out in what might seem a mild way, it brought on a confrontation and threatened the relationship. Wayne and Melissa took their two-year-old son to their country house every weekend. Wayne was busy for hours at a time, pursuing gardening and other projects around the house. Melissa was angry to begin with that he never talked to her about his schedule for the day and seemed not to want to spend time with his very active son. But then one day she didn't even know where he was. He went into the woods behind their house looking for firewood and came back two hours later. She was furious, she said, because he had no respect for her needs or her feelings. He did whatever he wanted, whenever he wanted, and she had no free time at all. She felt so angry she thought about leaving him.

Melissa's preconceived idea of how they would raise their son was that they would participate as equal partners, but Wayne's idea was that he would do the "manly" chores and she would take care of the child. They had discussed this disagreement before, and Wayne had said he would change. Thus when he disappeared into the woods, Melissa was furious and felt nothing would ever change. Disappearing into the woods is a mild form of acting-out, compared to having an affair or being physically abusive to your mate, but it caused serious repercussions because it symbolized a lack of communication and trust.

Melissa expected that her husband would share equally in child-care and would tell her of his plans. Another woman might not expect this and thus might not be as upset. But if you do not expect much from your man, you also will not get much. If your man acts out and it upsets you, then it is a problem whether he agrees or not. You need to understand why it upsets you and work on the issue with him. You are not making a big deal out of nothing.

Let's look now at what you can do when he acts out, mildly or severely, after you have a child.

TOUGH AND TENDER TALK

The Tough and Tender Talk will help you to maintain your separateness from his destructive actions while still communicating to him that you want change. This approach takes practice. In the first section of this approach, you talk to yourself (or a friend or therapist). In the second part, you talk to him. Although you need to feel tough and may even sound that way, what you say and do is tender and caring because you are trying to save and improve your life with him.

In the first part, you talk to yourself. Don't skip this part and start yelling at him. You need to know what his deeper reasons are for acting out, and you need to have a strategy and air out your own feelings. In the second step you talk to him.

Here is the Tough and Tender Talk approach for dealing with his acting-out behavior:

Talk to Yourself

First, convince yourself that he has unconscious feelings that are making him act this way. Determine in your mind what those invisible, unconscious emotions are. Listen to your intuitive sense about him and look at his family history.

Second, convince yourself that screaming at him or crying will not help. Of course you feel furious or anxious or scared or any other number of feelings. Find someone (a friend or therapist) to ventilate to about your feelings so you can deal with the situation calmly.

Talk to Him

First, tell him what he is doing that you consider to be acting-out behavior. Tell him what you feel toward him. Tell him what feelings you think he is having that are causing him to act out, *if* he is interested in hearing this. (You will need to explain what "acting-out" is to begin with: actions taken to avoid having and expressing feelings.) If he verbally attacks you, don't tell him about his feelings. Do not yell or become apologetic.

Second, tell him specifically what change you want from him and what changes you are willing to make. Don't hold back from telling him what negative effect you think his behavior will have on your child, or on your relationship with him, if he doesn't change. He may feel guilty or anxious as a result, but these feelings may push him to seek help.

If you're thinking of leaving him, try this strategy first. Threatening a man with leaving can often be a very effective way to get him to change, but you should only say this when you are serious. Remember that back in chapter three we looked at several ways you can threaten to leave without actually leaving. These, too, can make him aware of how serious you are. Look again at that section if you feel like leaving him. Physical violen ce, as we said, requires immediate action—getting help or separating.

There is nothing wrong if he feels guilty because his acting-out is harming the child and harming their future relationship. Guilt can be an effective tool in motivating him to change. Although he will most likely be angry because you make him feel guilty, you are actually doing him a tremendous favor in trying to prevent future problems and saving his relationship with his child.

Of course you're not perfect and you may be adding to the problems he has being a good father and mate. At the end of this section you'll find a checklist to assess without self-blame whether or not you might be part of the reason he's acting this way.

APPLYING THE TOUGH AND TENDER TALK APPROACH TO HIS ACTING-OUT

Now let's see how this works with the real acting-out problems that were listed above:

He Repeatedly Messes up When He's Taking Care of Your Child

Michael and Kristine have been married for five years. Four years ago they had their son, Marc. Kristine tells us about the problem.

"We both have to work to make ends meet, so we agreed that Michael would take care of Marc equally with me. Since we both work for the phone company, we were able to juggle our schedules so that we wouldn't work too often at the same time and one of us could be with Marc. Family Day Care provides the rest of the help. Housework was also supposed to be shared jointly.

"Michael does take care of Marc half the time, but nothing ever seems to go right. The Family Day Care Center calls me all the time because Michael is late to pick up Marc. When they finally get home and I call, Marc seems to be crying a lot because he's hungry and Michael hasn't gotten his dinner yet or there's been a fight about taking a bath or going to bed. I feel anxious worrying about what's happening at home, and I'd quit my job if we didn't need the money. The house has also become a mess because Michael isn't doing his share to clean as he promised."

Kristine talks to herself:

First, I think Michael's more upset than he realizes that I don't stay at home and take care of everything the way his mother did.

He's acting this way unconsciously to get me to take care of everything, even though he knows we need my income. I think he's also acting like his father, inept and incompetent even though he's really more competent than that.

Second, I hate him when he makes excuses and doesn't take care of Marc very well. It makes me furious at him when he acts this way.

Kristine talks to Michael:

First, I can tell him that he's acting-out when he is late all the time to pick up Marc, make him dinner, and so on. And I'll say that it reminds me of what he's said about his own father. I think he's late or messes up handling Marc because unconsciously he's upset that I'm not there to take care of Marc and this way tells me I ought to be there. I'll also tell him that I think he feels insecure and anxious about how to handle Marc because his father was not good at it either. There's nothing wrong with feeling anxious. If he acknowledges it, he could feel better and get some help.

Second, I'm going to tell him that either I have to quit my job and stay home with Marc, or we need to spend more money on a babysitter to take over when I'm working. In either case, Michael has to find some way to make more money. Otherwise he has to be on time and try harder to be patient with Marc. I want him to take parenting courses or join a fathers' support group I heard of. Marc is beginning not to trust him. He feels he can't count on dad to make him feel safe. If Michael doesn't get some help and stop acting-out, Marc could be messed up later on.

He Takes on New Interests and Projects, So That He Is Rarely with You and Your Child.

Sheila talks about Paul. "We have two children, ages three and six, so our life is difficult anyway. But Paul is so self-centered it makes me crazy! Of all the times to decide to go back to school, he picked the year after our second child was born. I appreciate that he wants to get a degree, but this is the wrong time. The kids need him and so do I, but we see him only on Sunday for a few hours. Then it's back to the books! Saturday he's at school and a few nights a week, too. He says he's doing it for our future, but I'm suspicious.

"I think he's overdoing this because he doesn't like being with us. At school he feels like he's young and a free spirit. It's costing us a lot of money for him to go to school, money we could use for childcare. I've tried to go along with his plan, but being with the kids without his help is making me too impatient and not a good mother. Something's got to change."

Sheila talks to herself:

First, if I look at his going to school as acting-out, I think the unconscious emotions that made him take on this project right now are: he's afraid of being home with us because he's afraid he'll be like his father who was explosive and violent. Also, Paul needs to feel in control, to feel good about himself. He feels I'm in charge of the home, so he doesn't want to be here and feel second in command. And I think he feels angry about being grown up and caring for a family.

Second, knowing this makes me feel even more angry and hopeless, too.

Sheila talks to Paul:

First, it won't help to tell him about his father because he gets so furious if I ever talk about his family. But I will tell him that I think he's going to school now because he's angry and frustrated dealing with me and the kids. And that the kids feel rejected. And that I need him here to help me be a better mother.

Second, I will ask him to take only one course next term and to make a schedule with me of when he'll be with the kids. I'm willing to hold back from telling him what to do when he's with the kids if that will help him feel in control. And I'm willing to look at my need to control our household if he'll spend more time pitching in. I want him to go for therapy to talk about his feelings about being a father, but I don't think he'll go.

He Won't Get a Better-Paying Job Even Though You Need the Money. He Loses His Job or Causes Problems at Work That Jeopardize Job.

Dana tells about Bob. They have a three-and-a-half-year-old child and another on the way. "I can only work part-time and Bob works by himself as a carpenter. But he doesn't drum up business and work is sporadic, so we don't have enough money. He could work for a construction firm, where his income would be more stable. Or he could try to get more work, start his own company with some guys he knows. He says money isn't that important and I'm being middle-class. But what's middle-class about being able to pay the rent and the health insurance? That's just barely surviving. He grew up in a middle-class family and so did I, and I don't see what's wrong with that. In fact, Bob likes to spend money more than I do."

Dana talks to herself:
First, Bob doesn't want to make money, and I see this now as a form of acting-out. The feelings underneath this are, I think, connected to his mother, who controls him by making him feel guilty. She never has money either, and I think Bob's afraid to make money because he thinks he'll have to take care of her. Bob blames me for being controlling when it's really his mother he should be angry at. He never expresses any feelings but shows me how angry he is by not trying to make more money. I think Bob also feels very insecure and anxious about dealing with clients but won't admit it. He hides behind this stuff about "middle-class" so he doesn't have to deal with his anxiety.

Second, I feel scared about our future, worried that we could become homeless. And I'm furious that still another burden is going to fall on me—supporting the family. I'm responsible for the kids and the house now and I'm managing our finances. Bob's not going to take that over if I work full-time. But I know when I yell at him about this stuff we don't get anywhere.

Dana talks to Bob:

First, what I'd like to say is that he's jeopardizing our relationship blaming me because we need more money to support ourselves and the kids. He's in an unconscious battle for control with his mother by not making more money. But we're the ones who are losing out. I'll also tell him that our children are going to have a rougher time of it than we have if he doesn't deal with his money problems now.

Second, I want Bob to deal with his issues about making money in therapy or another group. I don't want to have to be the primary wage earner, not with two young children. So I want him to take on more responsibility for making money. If he absolutely won't do that, then he has to take on more childcare and household tasks, such as shopping, cooking, making doctor's appointments, and so on, every day.

He Gets Sick More Often, Has Accidents, Gets Himself into Trouble Legally, or Loses Things All the Time.

Jean is very anxious about David. She tells us:

"David's always been a bit of a hypochondriac and complains more than I do if he even gets a cold. And he's forever bumping his head or cutting himself accidentally. And of course he wants a lot of attention for these things. But since Jessica was born five years ago, David's been worse. He badly sprained his ankle when I came home from having Jessica. I had to take care of him when I was the one who had just had a baby. Then he got shingles, which is supposedly as a result of anxiety, when Jessica turned one. He was sick for a while with that.

"When she was two, he got hit by a car when biking in the park.

It wasn't really his fault, but he wasn't in the bike lane and made a turn without looking. He was only scratched up, but it scared me. When Jessica turned three he fell off a ladder cleaning a gutter outside the house. He was in bed for two weeks and still has trouble with his back. But he doesn't go for help. He just complains.

"I'm worried that the next time he has an accident or gets sick he won't recover. It always happens around her birthday, and she's about to turn five. He complained of chest pains at her birthday last year. And I know a man who had a stroke recently. He was only forty-one also, just like David. What if he can't work for a long while, or he dies?"

Jean talks to herself:

First, it's been hard for me to see that these accidents and illnesses are because of unconscious emotions and aren't just bad luck, but the pattern is getting very obvious. Obviously David wants to be taken care of. But it's more than that. He's desperately anxious for attention and furious if he doesn't get it, because of his childhood. His mother ignored him. She expected him to be the perfect gentleman unless he was really sick or hurt. Yet his sister was spoiled and still is. David should be angry about this because his mother was unfair. But he protects her and won't see what she's really like. Instead he acts out and continues to have these physical problems.

Second, I'm feeling impatient and don't want to be sympathetic anymore to his accidents and illnesses. Between taking care of a child and David, I've got my hands full. I'm angry at him and a nervous wreck waiting for his next catastrophe. Sometimes I wish he would just die so we'd get the insurance money and I wouldn't have to worry about him. I do still love him though.

Jean talks to David:

First, I know you're not getting sick and having accidents on purpose, but it's not just bad luck. You make me into your mother and Jessica into your sister and think this is the only way to get me to take care of you. But I'm not your mother and Jessica's your daughter. One day something really serious could happen to you if you don't deal with this. And it's bad for Jessica to see her father getting hurt a lot and getting attention for it. I love you and want to pay attention to you, but without your getting sick.

Second, I want you to go for individual therapy or I'll go with you so we can talk about this issue between us. I don't blame you if you want to be taken care of, but you've got to recognize that you unconsciously want to get sick or hurt. Otherwise something really bad may happen to you. Tell me directly that you want my attention, even when I'm involved with Jessica. And let me know if you're angry that I'm preoccupied. This would also help me to separate from Jessica. I also want Jessica to have a chance to be closer to you.

He Has an Affair or a Serious Flirtation.

Hilary is distraught about her marriage. "Recently I found out by accident that Charles, my husband, has been seeing someone he used to date. Our son was born six months ago, and I didn't have time to notice how distant Charles seemed. I noticed he was preoccupied when we were together although he's very happy with the baby. We didn't have sex like we used to, but I figured we were both exhausted from the baby anyway. Now I know why he wasn't interested. I've already confronted him with this. He admits he's been seeing this woman but says that it just happened, he doesn't know why, and it's over. That's not good enough for me, but I don't know what else to do except leave him—and I don't want to do that."

Hilary talks to herself:
First, I don't want to bother figuring out anything about Charles. But I will if I have to. His father had affairs, so he's doing what his father did. Also, his mother has been very sick for the past year,

and he's really scared that she might die. And I'm not there for him the way I used to be either. I guess the idea of losing the two most important women in his life made him terrified. I feel sorry for him, but sorrier for myself. He also turned thirty-five this year and doesn't feel he's as successful as he ought to be by now. He probably wanted someone to boost his ego.

Second, what I feel toward him is rage. I want to kill him. And I feel horribly hurt that he did this to me and to our family. And I feel confused and that I don't love him anymore. I'm going to therapy because I have to have someone to talk to.

Hilary talks to Charles:

First, I have told him how furious I am and that I'm thinking about separating for a while, but the baby stops me. I'm going to tell him all the unconscious reasons why I think he did this: imitating his father, his fear that his mother and I were not going to be there for him anymore, his success issues. And I'll tell him that the only way he's going to stop acting-out is if he works at becoming aware of his real feelings so he doesn't act on them.

Second, of course I expect him to stop seeing this woman and never do this again. But we have to go for couples' therapy or he has to go alone to find out for himself why he did this. He has to do this in order for me to trust that he's serious about getting to the root of this acting-out. If he has complaints about me, I'm willing to hear them if they're constructive and he wants to work on our relationship.

He Suddenly Begins Drinking to Excess or Takes Drugs. He Becomes Physically Aggressive, even Violent, with You or Child.

Nadine talks about Eddie. "It's awful to be scared of the man you live with, but that's my life now. Before we had Pamela, he wasn't as bad as he has been this year. Occasionally we'd have an argument and he'd push me away from him because I wouldn't let up on him. But he started drinking with his buddies after work, and he comes home once a week high. Fighting with him then is dangerous. Pamela's learned to stay away from him when he's like that. I have to learn the same thing because the more I yell at him about being drunk, the worse he gets. He's pushed me hard a few times, twisted my arm, and kicked me during a fight. Pamela hasn't seen him be violent, but she hears the yelling and starts to cry.

"Eddie never used to drink very much when we were dating. I saw him get drunk for the first time at our wedding. Then we had Pamela unexpectedly a year later. Fatherhood and marriage has done something to him and we need help before I get hurt and Pamela starts to have real problems because of the fighting."

Nadine talks to herself:

First, Eddie's family drinks beer and overeats. They're all overweight, and I know that's an inherited tendency. He has two uncles that I heard were alcoholics. So part of this comes from his family. He doesn't show anger much—just gets silent and moody—and all those stored up feelings come out when he drinks and loses control of himself. I know his father used to hit the kids, though nobody talks about it much. I think most important he inherited feelings of resentment from his father about being responsible for a family. In other words, the way he thinks a father is supposed to feel is annoyed, put-upon, and overworked. Eddie, like me, needs his own space but doesn't know how to get it. He also deep down doesn't think much of himself. He's too connected to his father, who really was a failure, even though Eddie is not.

Second, I hate him when he's drinking. It just makes me furious and I can't seem to stop myself from jumping all over him (verbally). I really wish he were dead at those times. I feel like screaming, mostly because I'm scared and frustrated. My raging at him gets me into trouble because he gets physical.

Nadine talks to Eddie:

First, what I should tell him when he's sober is that he's getting drunk to avoid feeling anger, insecurity, and anxiety; and that he's endangering his relationship with me and with his daughter. And that this violent behavior when he's angry and drunk is acting-out all the feelings he keeps buried every day about everything that goes on here. He has to learn to express himself all the time—and not when he's drunk. I will tell him that I think his drinking and violent behavior was learned from his family, especially his father, and that it can't be part of our way of living.

Second, what I want from Eddie is for him to stop drinking altogether and to go to AA for help. I've started going to Al-Anon meetings (that's for the relatives and friends of alcoholics) to help me stay away from him when he's drunk and/or violent. I'm also going to tell him that if he doesn't stop all this and get some help for himself, I'm going to leave him. Living this way is too upsetting and dangerous for all of us.

A PEP TALK

While you are working on your mate to stop acting-out, remember that you are trying to get him to change patterns that have certainly been in his family for a long time, or that he learned unconsciously as a child. There is no harder job. As Drs. Cowan and Cowan remind us, when two people come from different backgrounds, negative cycles are more likely to be repeated if they come through the husband's family line rather than the wife's.

You are doing a tremendously important job by attempting to change negative cycles both for your family now and for the families that will evolve from yours in the future. Once your man stops acting-out, he will most likely become more involved with you and with the children—something that all families need from the father. And you can tell him that being involved is better for him, too. In the study *When Partners Become Parents*, it was found that "more involved fathers continue to have lower parenting stress and report fewer symptoms of depression."

You need a pat on the back. Use the pep talk ideas in chapter two and talk back to your fears. Here are some other thoughts to encourage you in your work with him:

1. Acting-out hurts everyone in the family, the children as well as me. It will not go away unless I address his problems directly.
2. I should give myself tremendous credit for dealing with these issues instead of burying my head in the sand. I have courage and strength.
3. I am choosing neither to live a life of quiet frustration and suffering nor to leave him without first making an effort to get him to change. This is teaching my children not to stand for destructive behavior, and putting some effort into a relationship that is important.

And one last thought. Men act out because of all kinds of events, not just because they have a child. For example, Phyllis went back to school two nights a week after being a full-time housewife for many years. Her husband was used to having her at home with him every night. Within the first month her husband broke his arm while cooking himself dinner while she was at school. In this way, he acted out his feelings about her leaving him alone at night. The ideas and skills you learn here for dealing with his acting-out behavior will come in handy throughout your life with him, not just after you have a child.

HOW CAN I IMPROVE?

The psychoanalyst Dorothy Dinnerstein wrote that, "woman . . . will remain fitted for this role as half-human 'other,' and can never escape it, as long as she agrees to go on being the goddess of the nursery." You don't want to be "goddess" of the nursery, but you want to protect your child from harm, and society tells you that as a mother you are responsible. So you take charge because someone has to and no one else is volunteering. In this section, you can reexamine your position in the "nursery" and in other areas, using the following questions. There are ways in which you can let go or make changes that would free you and help your man to improve as well.

It is extremely important that you do not blame yourself for any changes you see that you need to make. You are not at fault. Instead, you deserve credit for trying to improve your life and your family's. The questions are to help you think differently about how you live now. There are no right or wrong answers.

Self-Evaluation Questions

1. Am I yelling too much out of frustration at him or at my child (every day, for instance, or more)? But I'm not getting help for myself?
2. Do I try to figure out what I actually feel toward my mate and tell him (instead of going on about how awful he is)?
3. Do I try to figure out what I feel toward my child every day, instead of yelling or giving orders or holding everything in? Do I at times tell my child what he is making me feel, whether it is angry feelings or loving ones, when it is appropriate? (Angry feelings are a normal and necessary part of motherhood.)
4. Do I actually ask my mate to do specific tasks, or sit down with him and divide up the work?
5. Do I think I have to take care of everything or nothing will get done right (and there will be a disaster)? Would it really be so bad if certain things did not get done right?
6. Do I correct my child and my mate about actions that are really not that important? Is this part of the reason they keep thinking of me as "boss"? Could I do this less?
7. Do I try to figure out what my mate or my children do in the

moment that upsets me? Do I try to tell them right then (instead of letting the feelings spill out at an inappropriate time)?

8. Do I hold onto anger and resentment after I've gotten what I wanted?

9. Do I work on my issues as I want my mate to work on his? Do I know what in my past might affect me negatively today as a mother and a companion?

10. Do I have control issues with my man about my child? Do I always think "His way is wrong," instead of, "His way is different from mine and he needs to establish his own relationship with our child"?

11. Do I hold everything in until I'm ready to explode—and then do?

12. Have I studied how my mate provokes me? Am I trying not to allow myself to be provoked into an explosion (especially one in front of the children) because explosions do not help?

13. Do I ignore his acting-out or emotional issues because I am scared of discussing the problems? Am I fooling myself in hoping that he will change without my intervention?

14. Am I so dependent on my mate that this encourages him to think he can mistreat me? Do I avoid developing an independent life for myself?

One of the harder decisions to make each day is when to take control of your child and your home, and when to let go. When to work on your man to change his acting-out behavior, and when to step back, detach from his problems, and find a way to live your life as well as possible even though he acts out. AA and the other twelve-step programs for addictions use the Serenity Prayer to guide members in realizing that there are some situations they can change and some situations they cannot change. They hope for the "wisdom to know the difference." But there is no handbook that can tell you exactly when you've worked enough at a problem and when you should let go. Knowing your "bottom line" can help, however.

KNOWING YOUR BOTTOM LINE

How long do you work on your mate to get him to stop acting-out before you give up? You are the only one who can make that decision. We know that change is slow, but that difficult men can change.

During the time that you work on the problems, be aware of your bottom line. Your bottom line is the point beyond which you are ready to break up the relationship. A bottom line can be extremely effective to use as a threat that spurs your mate into action, *if* you are serious.

But here are some rules: Don't make a decision to separate in the midst of a heated argument. Especially when you have children, a decision about breaking up has to be thought out carefully and apart from the anger of the moment. *Always* seek help for yourself, and try to get help as a couple for one to two years before deciding to break up.

The physically dangerous form of acting-out, violent behavior, should be every woman's bottom line. No one can or should tolerate, for any period of time, physically dangerous behavior, including aggression that places your child in danger. Once you and your child are not physically threatened, you can work on the issues with him in therapy as a couple, if he'll agree, or go by yourself.

When you hate your man or feel hurt because he acts out, it is a very frustrating, difficult, and painful experience to stay with him to work on the issues. But when you do confront the issues, you will be providing a wonderful role model for your child of a woman who has the confidence to approach her mate with courage and intelligence to try and motivate him to change. And you are demonstrating that although you are furious, hurt, and anxious, you still have the emotional flexibility to work with your difficult man toward eliminating his acting-out behavior.

If your man does change, he will make the most important contribution of his life to his children and give them an invaluable gift for their future: That a man, because he cares enough, can change and by so doing dramatically improve his family's life in the present, and for generations to come.

NINE

Two Steps Forward, One Step Back: The Slow Progress of Difficult Men and How You Can Survive the Struggle and Thrive

Women's lives offer valuable models because of the very pressures that make them seem more difficult.

—MARY CATHERINE BATESON

D_o *any* modern women find happiness in their relationships with their men? The answer is a definite yes. And it is not because they have found the perfect mate who says and does just what they want, one who requires no work. There are no perfect men. Waiting for the perfect man is clearly not the answer to finding happiness in a relationship.

We need to look further to understand what makes for happiness for a modern woman in a relationship. The answer became clearer as I walked and talked with a psychologically astute friend, Rhoda. She has been married to Donald for many years. We were commiserating about the tough times we and so many women have gone through with our men. Suddenly, however, Rhoda stopped short and said, "Yet Donald tells me all the time how happy he is and how wonderful his life is because of me. He says he owes everything to me." And I quickly added, "That makes all the difference in the world, doesn't it? It makes all the work and arguing worthwhile." Rhoda vehemently agreed. She added that knowing how much he appreciated her made the maddening times with him so much easier to take.

Then there is Miriam, who told me that her fiancé, Bob, doesn't mind telling friends and family how she saved his life years before when she forced him (with threats of leaving) to enter a drug program. And in fact he has told me the same thing, adding that he owed his life to her tough stand with him. Miriam said she continues to feel appreciated by Bob, which keeps her going despite the hard times they still weather.

We have all heard famous men, politicians especially, make public statements praising the "little woman" for helping them get where they are when they have arrived at a position of importance. That praise tells us nothing about what the women actually mean to them. But when Rhoda and Miriam tell us what their men have said about them, the message is clear: their importance is not based on ironing shirts or smiling at business functions. Their men have been able to admit what an important emotional and intellectual impact their women have had on them. The men have acknowledged the emotional work and risks the women have had to take to get through to them about vital relationship issues. And we can hear how important it has been for the relationships, and for Miriam's and Rhoda's good feelings about themselves, that their men regularly "testify" to their importance in this way.

The answer, then, to finding happiness with a man, is to first understand that all relationships take work. And then to find a man whom you love and who loves you whose issues you decide for yourself are ones that you do not mind working on. The man must of course be with you for the "long haul"; he must be there to hear what you have to say even if he doesn't comply for months or even years. He will often think you are wrong or crazy or demanding or critical or controlling.

But deep down he knows differently. And he can change when he wants to or perhaps finally when you are fed up. Slowly he changes in small ways. And at first occasionally, and then more often, and perhaps about the wrong topic, he appreciates you. And he says it. And his changing improves your life. Your efforts have not been in vain. He may forget how much he appreciates you during the next fight. But he remembers the next day.

This is the kind of man with whom a woman finds happiness. Cinderella, Snow White, and Sleeping Beauty only find their princes in storybooks and on movie screens. If you wait for a Cinderella life to start, you will have wasted your life. Miriam and Rhoda have found real-life happiness with their difficult, far-from-perfect men. Each one's life with her mate is in fact a work in progress, important enough to be described in any national magazine, just as any other work of art in progress might be. Because a fulfilling lifelong relationship between two equal partners is really a work of art. Perhaps it's because women's work has always been taken for granted that we have ignored the vital contribution women make when trying to get through to their men to improve their relationships.

Right now, however, you may not be seeing any progress in your work of art. You feel stuck and discouraged. Let's see if there are ways to make yourself feel better.

CLOSE SCRUTINY YIELDS A RICHNESS OF SMALL CHANGES

The work of a relationship is as frustrating as any other creative work—writing a novel, painting, composing. In the beginning stages it looks as if nothing is happening and nothing ever will develop. You feel like giving up or wish that you had never begun. You are trying hard but nothing is coming out as you planned. Yet closer scrutiny of the scribbling on the pieces of paper or wet paint on a canvas shows that there are ideas that will lead to a book or finished painting.

A closer examination of your relationship and your man can similarly yield a richness of small steps which are the beginning of big changes. These are to your credit because you have been the catalyst. Here then is a way to feel better about yourself and about him when it feels as if nothing has improved. You will be your own best friend who tells you: "Things seem to be better between you. He was so much more_____last night than he used to be." Here's a list of the kind of small changes you can look for that you might otherwise ignore. They are often fleeting occurrences that require an objective and alert eye.

1. He holds his temper in a situation where he would normally explode. (Although the next time he may yell again.)

2. He is verbally supportive of you about a problem at work or a problem with your child, when he usually is silent or critical.
3. He buys the gift you said you wanted for your birthday. In the past he would get you something awful or nothing at all.
4. He gets cards and flowers for you for Mother's Day (or makes sure the children do this). Even if you had to make a point of telling him he had better not forget, he's still able to give you something without a power struggle. Previously he forgot or ruined the day.
5. He starts to do the dishes regularly, as you had discussed. Even if he does them hours later than you would like, it's still an important step in the right direction.
6. Without prompting, he asks you, "How was your day?" and then listens to what you say. (You've told him several times that you want to know he's interested and that he should ask.)
7. He speaks up in a conflict situation (in a store or restaurant, for example, or at home with workmen or during a problem with your child) and helps to resolve the issue where he usually stays silent.

You deserve to be praised and you *should* praise yourself for these small changes that you see. If you did not complain about these issues and ask for these changes, they would never occur. And always thank him for what he's done or tell him how terrific he is. However, *don't* gloat. Do *not* say:

- "You see how easy that was. Don't you feel better about yourself?"
- "I told you that you could do that."
- "That was great. I hope's it's not the last time you do this."
- "It's just because I asked you to do . . . that you did it for me. Let's see if you ever do . . . without my asking."

Comments such as these will leave him feeling resentful, worthless, inadequate, and back in the power struggle with you. Of course you want to say "I told you so," but it won't help. Although he's making

small changes, he's not feeling confident enough to be able to acknowledge that you're helping him, and he is most likely angry
about pleasing you, even though he is trying. He's not ready to give
you this type of appreciation that admits that he needs help in
certain areas.

Ask him, however, for appreciation about other areas in which
you are thoughtful and taking care of the business of your life together. Get the support and appreciation you deserve about the
emotional work you are putting into him (and the work you are
putting into yourself) from other sources—such as good friends or
a therapist—that are conflict-free in relation to you.

But you feel you need more than this and you're right. He is not
giving you what you need, and you're exhausted from the many jobs
you do as wife, companion, professional woman, and possibly
mother, too. You need a physical and emotional boost to have the
energy to keep going.

An Energy Theory

Perhaps you have a friend who has constant energy or you have
admired a famous woman (Jane Fonda, for example) who has it all,
including the problems, but still has the energy of ten women. You
wonder why your own energy level is perpetually below zero. You
manage to do what needs to be done for your man or child or job,
but you are left with little for yourself. The reason why you are
"running on empty" will be clearer if you understand that your
physical well-being is determined not only by how much you have
to do during the day, but what you are getting out of all this "doing."
To help further understand this, let's look at what I call the Human
Energy Theory.

The Human Energy Theory is explained this way: Your energy
increases with the increase of "feeding" to your ego. Flattering experiences, enjoyable activities, soothing and supportive relationships, work that is stimulating and rewarding—all of these "feed"

your ego in a nourishing form, resulting in an increase in your energy. When these elements are missing in your life, your energy will decrease.

When you are spending your day working on him, even though it is in order to get what you want, you need more than ever to take time and give yourself the kind of flattering or soothing experiences you need to have more energy. Women are especially used to self-sacrifice. You spend your day feeding your man or your child's ego, sacrificing activities and relationships that would make you feel more alive, more energetic. And if your man is critical or your job is anxiety-provoking or your child has a bad day, you are definitely not being fed but are being drained. The energy theory says that you will feel exhausted—and you do.

Patsy, for example, thought there had to be something seriously wrong with her because all she wanted to do was sleep. Yet with a one-year-old son who often awoke in the middle of the night and a full-time job as an office manager, she had little time to get the sleep she craved. She felt exhausted every day. Her doctor found nothing wrong with her. Her husband, Fred, couldn't understand how she could be so tired. He had plenty of energy to exercise and play tennis. Her problem, he said, was that she didn't get enough exercise. But she was too tired to exercise, even if she could somehow make the time to do it.

Patsy's job was all right, but she felt bored and underpaid there. She saw an ad for an office manager at a school of design, and on the spur of the moment, she applied. As part of the job she could take courses in design (tuition free), something she had always dreamed of. Patsy felt more excited than she had in a long time when she got the job. Fred was silent about her decision to change jobs. She knew he thought she was taking a risk changing jobs "for no reason."

From the moment she started at the job, Patsy felt her tiredness melt away. Instead of wanting to sleep, she wanted to read or work on assignments for her course, although she was still tired out on those nights when her son was up a lot. She met some new friends at the school who also had children, and they became a support group for Patsy. She began to realize that Fred wasn't doing enough at home to take the burden off of her, and she felt furious at first. She told Fred that she wanted him to share the job of going into their son at night and to do the dishes if she cooked. He was annoyed but agreed. Patsy noticed that now Fred began to be too tired to exercise.

Although Patsy loved her son and husband, their needs drained her without replenishing her. Her husband especially was unsympathetic to her dreams, and her job gave her even less back. She kept all her anger suppressed and did not ask her husband for help. Of course she would feel continually tired. But her energy level changed when she found a field of work that was made for her, and when she found friends who were supportive and fun.

Every physical problem you have should, of course, be examined by a doctor. But while you're examining the physical causes of your fatigue, think about the energy theory. Are you getting enough of what you need emotionally to help you feel alive and happy and full of life? Most women aren't. We all need the following "New Creed."

A NEW CREED FOR MODERN WOMEN

When you are involved with a difficult man, which means any man, it is easy to stop taking care of yourself. You're busy trying to communicate with him, trying to understand what he does and why. He seems more important than you are. Although we have focused on your man and your feelings toward him throughout this book, your own well-being should be your first concern. To convince you of this, here is the "New Creed for Modern Women," a belief system to replace the old rules that taught women that self-sacrifice and martyrdom were signs of love. These statements are designed to do battle with the internal tapes that get you to deprive yourself.

Playwright and actress Cornelia Otis Skinner said, "Women keep a special corner of their hearts for sins they have never committed." There is unfortunately too much truth in Ms. Skinner's caustic comment. Too many women feel this deep sense of "sin" or wrongdoing which is not based in reality and has nothing to do with who they truly are. Yet because you carry around this sense of being wrong, you work extra hard for others in order to justify feeling good about yourself. The result is that you neglect yourself.

You need this New Creed to remind you that you are entitled to enjoy your life. By taking care of yourself, you will ultimately help all your relationships as well. Here, then, are several statements that you can use to maintain your resolve to put yourself first whenever you can, and to keep your energy high on your own behalf, instead of on the behalf of your man.

A New Creed for Modern Women

- I deserve to feel as good as I make others feel.
- If I do more good things for myself, my stress level will be lower. Thus I will be ready to deal with problems constructively.
- When I take care of myself, I feel better and I'll be better able to deal with my difficult mate (and family).
- I'll have more physical and emotional energy.
- Feeling good about myself won't depend on whether he or others give me what I want and need.
- Relationships improve when each person takes responsibility for making themselves happy.
- I enjoy time alone. I deserve time alone. I need it.
- I deserve to feel good each day, even if I have done nothing at all for others that day. I deserve to feel good because I am me.
- I will be a good role model for my mate. He may learn to take care of himself by watching me. He will respect me more because I think enough of myself to take care of myself well.

And for Mothers:

- I'll be a better role model for my child if I take care of myself well. Children do what you do, not what you say.

- Because mothering requires the greatest output of energy and nurturance, I must especially make my good emotional and physical health a requirement.
- If I have another job outside the home too, making time for myself is even harder but a great necessity.
- When I make my well-being a priority, I am a better mother.

You will need to repeat relevent portions of the New Creed for Modern Women to yourself every day until you have overcome your tendency to neglect yourself. But even when you are convinced that taking care of yourself is important, your man may not agree. After all, time you spend on yourself will not be spent on him. Let's see how you can use the New Creed to combat any unconscious sabotage by your mate.

SABOTAGE AND YOUR MAN

Joan spent hours talking to Steve, her boyfriend, about his problems with his children. They usually talked when they met after work. But Joan decided she needed to take an exercise class to help her lose weight, and that class met after work, too. She told Steve that three days a week she would be exercising, but they could get together after her class. Although he said that was fine, he began to play pool several nights a week so that he was unavailable when Joan was free. In order to see Steve, Joan stopped going to her exercise class. He stopped playing pool as much.

Joan was in group therapy and one of the other members pointed out that Steve was unconsciously sabotaging Joan. Since she wasn't going to be available for him when he wanted her, then he wouldn't be available for her when she wanted to be with him. Joan realized she was now sabotaging herself by not exercising.

She used the ideas of the New Creed to remind herself that she was entitled to lose weight and be healthier. Then, when she felt confident, she spoke to Steve about his feelings and about the "game" he was playing. He was able to acknowledge this, and they renegotiated a time when they could be together, including some time, though less than before, when he could talk about his children. Jane also became stronger in insisting that he find a therapist to talk to about these issues because his problems were preventing them from having a good time together.

When your man, consciously or not, sabotages you in your efforts to take better care of yourself and put yourself first, as Steve did to Joan, you especially need to use the New Creed. It will remind you that you are entitled to a separate nutrient life of your own—and it will remind your man as well. Steve was angry that Joan abruptly stopped their get-togethers. He was anxious, too, about being left alone with free time and with his problems with his children. He also felt insecure about their relationship. If Joan was going to look better, perhaps she would leave him.

As we have discussed before, men who are unable to identify or express their feelings, and who do not have self-awareness or insight show their feelings through actions, as Steve did by playing pool. The techniques we've discussed throughout this book will help you in communicating to your man what you think he is really feeling underneath his behavior.

But the New Creed is for *you.* Use it to keep yourself on course in making your well-being a priority above all else, especially when you're expending energy working on your difficult man to change in the relationship.

HOW WELL ARE YOU TAKING CARE OF YOURSELF?

Here's a questionnaire that you can use to evaluate whether or not you are taking care of yourself well. The questions are designed to make you critique the way you live your life in terms of eating well, exercising, finding time for yourself, surrounding yourself with the right kind of friends and job, and whether or not you let your relationship stand in the way of leading your own full and active life.

1. Are you exhausted every day without sufficient physical cause? (You should be checked by a doctor for any physical problems.) Could this exhaustion come from being emotionally depleted? Could it be because you are not being appreciated?

2. Does your job make you feel good? If not, is your man supportive of you in this situation? Does he support your finding a better job? Are you scared to leave anyway?

3. Do you think about how you prefer to spend your time and do it, or do your mate's needs take priority?

4. Do you continue giving to your man even though he does not give you anything back? (He may not give you what you give him, but he should, in some clear way, make you feel loved and cared about.)

5. Do you continue to pursue friends who do not reciprocate? Do you continue to give to people who are withholding after you realize this about them? Why?

6. Do you know the right way to eat but you don't follow this because your man (or others) does not support you to eat in a healthful way?

7. Do you exercise as much as you can each week, or do you say you don't have the time? Do you lack time because you are taking care of others? Do you lack time because you want to avoid friction with your mate about his taking on responsibilities at home?

8. If you are a mother (working outside the home or not), do you make sure to have some time to yourself every day?

9. If you are a mother, do you back down from getting childcare or having your mate be with your child because you feel you don't deserve time off? Or because your man is not supportive of your time off?

There can be numerous reasons why you don't take better care of yourself, why you don't put yourself first in your life. We know that there are many demands on your time. You make time to clean your house or play with a child or reorganize your man's closet, but at the end of this physical effort, you are exhausted and have no energy left to exercise. Mary Bateson tells us that "on the one hand, physical effort can be depleting. . . . On the other hand regular exercise leaves the feeling of having more available." Women are taught to expend their physical energy by taking care of others, which leaves them, as Ms. Bateson says, "depleted."

You may neglect yourself because in your childhood you were neglected or deprived in some way, taught to take care of others first, in general given a negative self-image so that you feel you don't deserve to have more. You may experience guilt, anxiety, and fear when you take the time to exercise, eat right, or just have an enjoyable evening with friends. Unconsciously you think that someone will disapprove. That "someone" may originally have been a parent; now the someone has become your man.

When you inhibit yourself because of fear of your mate's disapproval, it is not only your man's negativity that is inhibiting you. Your tendency to let someone else's disapproval stop you did not start with your relationship with him. Yes, he is in fact critical or silent when you put yourself first, but you are giving him the power to control you because of issues in your own background.

Since your fear of a loved one's disapproval did not start today, it is important that you seek out therapy to help you overcome the destructive messages that you were given long ago, and that are still controlling you now in the present with him and with others. Look back at the earlier chapter on fear, where the pep talk and three-step strategy, along with the New Creed, will help you to have the life you deserve.

Ego-Enhancing Activities for Every Woman

You're great at knowing what your man needs, or what your child needs, but what about what you need? You may have little experience knowing yourself because you haven't had the time, and now that you've fought for your own private time, no one is coming forward to tell you what you should do that will make you feel better in the small amount of time you've achieved for yourself. Here is a list of suggested activities that will enhance your ego and make you feel good about yourself even when your man is only causing you emotional pain. Choose the activities that are right for you and be unrelenting about holding onto your time.

1. Take aerobic walks a few times a week (and aimless strolling on alternate days).
2. Join a health club or exercise class. Go there even if you only have a half hour.
3. Decide on a project that you can accomplish for yourself (straightening your papers, writing anything at all, reading books you've always wanted to read) and do it each day, even if it's for as little as fifteen minutes.
4. Meditate or practice yoga. Have a massage.
5. Meet a friend for dinner or a play or lecture or sports activity.
6. Go to a movie or a museum alone in the afternoon.
7. Go back to school—either for a career or just for fun.
8. If you can't go back to school now, get the reading list for the course you're interested in and make time to read.
9. Pursue that hobby or creative endeavor you've been putting off—painting, singing, gardening, photography. Anything you enjoy is important enough to do!
10. See a nutritionist to help straighten out your eating habits and perhaps to get vitamin supplements. Follow the plan!

11. If you can't pursue a personal project that you have in mind because your life is too busy now (you have a child or other large responsibility), make a list of all your ideas for the project and continue to add to it. The ideas then will be there when you have the time.

Although it appears that we've gotten far afield from your difficult man, we are really on a close parallel course. To live, love, and have children with your man—to stay aware of the problems and work constructively on the issues for a better quality of life—you must stay strong. If you try to tackle the issues presented in the previous chapters without leading a separate life from your man that makes you feel good, you will quickly feel depressed, exhausted, low in self-esteem, and ultimately weak.

Here's an example. Sara had always enjoyed being out with friends, sang in a choir, and had an exercise partner who walked with her a few times a week. She was an elementary school teacher and loved her work. After she moved in with Bob, she dropped out of the choir and stopped going out with friends as often. Bob was reclusive. He didn't like to socialize and rarely went out after work—and then only to dinner.

Sara yelled at him, humored him, tried to cajole him, even tried to make deals to get him to go out with her. Yet even on her birthday he made the evening she planned very unpleasant: he said that going to a show was a waste of money. He said he worked hard enough during the week and that was enough for him. Sara became more depressed. She felt tired all the time and stopped her walking program. Her exercise partner got angry and yelled at her to take care of herself first and worry about Bob second. This was just what Sara needed, and she began to come out of her slump.

She now is back to her old routine of seeing friends, exercising, and singing in the choir. Even though Bob complains about her being out all the time, Sara feels terrific. An unexpected side benefit of taking care of herself first is that Bob has shown some interest in joining the choir.

TWO STEPS FORWARD, ONE STEP BACK

Two steps forward, one step back is the manner in which all change happens. It is the way negotiations for a peaceful settlement in the Middle East occur. It is the way children mature—one day grown up, the next day needing babying. It is the way cultural changes occur. For example, more men have moved forward as single parents with full custody and responsibility for children than ever before, yet married men still only manage to do 25 percent of the housework and childcare, even when both spouses are working.

Two steps forward and one step back is the way your man changes also. One day he realizes you're the best thing that ever happened to him and he wants to get married; the next day he thinks you're out to control him and destroy his independence. One day he does the dishes and vacuums without being asked; the next day he can't boil an egg or put his socks in the hamper. One day he enjoys his work and feels ambitious; the next day he wants to quit and blames you for being bourgeois and keeping him at his job. One day he's aware that it's not you he's angry at, it's really his boss or his mother. The next day he acts like you're public enemy number one.

Rapid movement forward, then hasty retreats—this is the nature of how all change occurs, and it is enough to make you feel frustrated and confused. Sociologists, anthropologists, and philosophers who look at how changes occur over centuries can certainly see the advances that women have achieved in their relationships in terms of equality and intimacy. But on a week-to-week basis, you'll need to remind yourself of the greater picture.

Sometimes you may be envious because it seems as if others have a more peaceful relationship than you do. But quiet on the outside doesn't mean that all is well. After years of seeing men and women alone, and together as couples, in my practice, it is clear to me that the outside picture that people present does not have anything to do with how happy they feel inside or how long their relationship will last. Couples who fight regularly very often stay together longer than those who rarely say an angry word. And too often a quiet relationship often means that the woman has chosen to remain silent on the issues that upset her.

Doris Lessing said, "The number of women prepared to stand up for what they really think, feel, experience, with a man they are in love with is still very small." But the numbers are getting larger every day. You are always taking an emotional risk when you ask your man to look at himself and change. But now you have an excellent chance of getting what you want from the man in your life, whereas before there was no chance at all. The emotional risk is never too large when you realize you are creating a better future for yourself. And it will seem even more worthwhile to take risks with your man today when you realize that you are creating a better future for those little girls who right now may believe in the Cinderella story, but who will all too soon be facing the real world of difficult men.